merging dimensions

THE OPENING PORTALS OF SEDONA

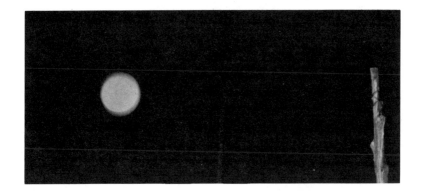

*Are these transitional anomalies
in Sedona, Arizona the beginning
of the future of mankind?*

Tom Dongo and Linda Bradshaw

Cover design by
Tom Dongo

Published by
Hummingbird Publishing
P.O. Box 2571
Sedona, AZ 86339

Sedona Color Graphics
■ ■ ▨ ■ PRINTING SPECIALISTS
Printed by Sedona Color Graphics

Contents

PART ONE — Linda Bradshaw

PART TWO — Tom Dongo

A Note From The Authors

The viewpoints of Linda Bradshaw and Tom Dongo presented in this book were written without collaboration. The two parts were written completely independently in order to give two different perspectives of an ongoing phenomenon by two participants.

▼

The photographs in this book:

• Were not retouched in any way,

• Were not altered in any manner except for the enlargement of specific objects on several photos,

• Are not a result of defects in the camera, film or developing process,

• Were not staged in any manner,

• Have no computer enhancement whatever.

Most of the photographs in this book were closely examined and processed by First Light Photo Lab, Sedona, Arizona.

All negatives are in the possession of the authors as proof of authenticity.

PART ONE
by Linda Bradshaw

Foreword

There is a wondrous place I wish to share with you. For obvious reasons I have omitted the actual location and will refer to it as Galactic Park throughout Part One of the book. My son originally coined the phrase, and in my opinion it aptly describes this enigmatic wonderland. The encounters I have been privileged to experience there have taken me on a journey like none other. As in all life, some of these experiences have been a bit traumatic and others have taken me to glorious heights of which I'd never known.

There have been a myriad of occurrences over the past two years, but I have chosen the most vivid of each type to share with you. These are not all that have occurred, nor have the experiences stopped. Within this time frame I compiled the following data and it is only now that I feel free to release it to the world.

This information is not intended to achieve any hidden agenda. It is only to inform those who wish to know. Perhaps it may appear a bit far-fetched to some, and for this, I will not apologize. This is merely truth and I cannot change the flavor or color of an experience to suit another's belief parameters. What is, is. To the best of my human ability I will share in exact detail all types of incidents that I have, to this point, experienced in relation to this fascinating area. These, I believe, are indicative of many things to come.

Join me on my journey. I share this with the fervent desire that each reader is inspired in a positive way.

Linda Bradshaw

Chapter 1

Galactic Park

The daylight brings with it an incredible beauty. The majestic red rocks of Sedona greet the morning sun, and the rolling hills sparkle as the birds sing their praises to life. The beauty here can, at times, take one's breath away. I have the feeling that I have been transported to another place and yet, I am still here on Earth. How privileged I am to be here.

Then the nighttime comes and all is still. There is often the feeling of a "presence." This presence is not completely discernible, yet there is just enough to put a person on alert. The sounds come and our dogs frantically bark their protests to the intruders. At other times these same dogs cower in a corner and whimper. What happened? What or who is here? In time I would realize that some of these "presences" appear during the daytime also.

My first initiation to this strange world began one evening when I chose to step outside to witness a meteor shower. It was particularly visible and very beautiful, but several lights shot directly sideways rather than downward, and they had a different intensity to them. My curiosity was piqued.

The following evening I drove to the highest point on a hill entering our ranch, which gives a direct view of the canyon these lights appeared to originate from; coincidentally, this same canyon was rumored to hide a secret military base. This bit of information only heightened my curiosity further.

I parked my pickup truck so that I could look out the driver's window directly toward the canyon. With camera aboard, I arrived at 8:00 and approximately half an hour later I observed an airborne vehicle of some sort with flashing red lights. It was approaching the canyon from a westerly direction. There was no sound to this aircraft. Many planes had passed over by this time, at the same altitude, and each time I could hear their motors or jet engines. This emitted no sound. Just prior to reaching the mouth of the canyon the vehicle began a quick descent, straight down, and as it was about to go below the horizon, a white streak (almost like a meteor) descended perpendicular to it. The white streak was just to the right of the craft. I waited for the craft to rise again, but it did not. Then, approximately 20 minutes later, at a mountain peak farther to the right (and deeper into the canyon) I again saw flashing red lights with no sound. These lights hovered above the peak for about five minutes and then suddenly began an ascent almost straight up; it was not a gradual ascent as a plane would take. This craft was not a helicopter. All through this exercise I shot pictures of the strange flying object.

Next, I saw what appeared to be a meteor in the sky, but instead of being all white, it was a bright red ball shooting across the sky with a white trail behind it (similar to a comet tail). It was not at a high altitude, and amazingly it shot out of the canyon and into the sky toward the west. It then disappeared almost instantly.

I was in the process of absorbing what I had just seen when something caught my attention to the left of and a little behind my truck. There, hovering just above a bush approximately 20 feet away, was a large ball of white light (perhaps four feet in diameter) which would dim and grow small, then gradually brighten and grow larger. It repeated this again and again: ball in the center with bright rays emitting out, then withdrawing and growing dim, all the time maintaining the small ball in the center. The pulse it emitted had the same cadence as a heartbeat.

The light was of an oyster-shell color. I instantly perceived an intelligence about it. There was no question in my mind that this was a life form of some sort. It was hovering directly above a bush approximately four feet high.

This took me aback somewhat, and as I quickly discerned the situation, I wanted to leave, but I also wanted a photo of the light. So be it. I would snap one photo then rush out of there. The plan sounded reasonable to me. I raised my camera, focused, and suddenly received a telepathic message that shot directly through me. An unseen voice told me, "Do not take one more picture." After a chill ran through me from head to toe, I placed the camera on the seat, started my truck, and raced down the hill to our ranch.

What happened next was almost as bizarre. The following day I took my film into town to be developed. The shots I had taken were the last 16 frames of a 36-exposure roll of high-speed film. My husband, Bob, is a photographer and he had used the front portion of the film for an advertising job. Knowing I was planning to do some night photos, he had saved the last part of the roll for me to use.

When I later picked up the photos I noticed that only the interior shots that Bob had taken were in the packet. I went back into the photo lab and asked if they had possibly thrown out some film that they thought had nothing on it. The man said, "There was some unused film that we threw out. It was blank." I asked to see the film and he brought me a completely blank strip of film. There wasn't even an indication of frames, which always show up whether the picture comes out or not. When I asked about this he agreed that if there had been any shots taken at all, at least the frames would have shown up on film. I took the blank film home and discussed this with my husband, who then called the lab to ask if it could possibly be a length of film that just didn't get developed. He was told that was impossible, as the machine they use takes the whole roll of film and develops it automatically. The lab technician then again stated that the roll was simply not used, ending the conversation with the statement that the camera must not have been activated.

The camera I use is a Kodak 635 that is fully automated. So this is not a case of forgetting to open the lens cover; the camera will not work if the cover is closed. The camera had clicked and automatically advanced 14 times. I shot 14 photos. When I first arrived on the hill that night, the counter showed 20 shots had been taken. It was a 36-exposure roll. When I returned home, it showed that a total of 34 photos had been taken, leaving two unused frames.

What happened to the film? Perhaps it was due to some sort of human intervention. I even thought of magnetic fields around the area, which might have erased the film, but if that were the case, all of the photos would have been eliminated, not just the ones I shot. Sedona, because of its iron-rich red rocks, has strong magnetic fields.

Initially I was devastated, because this was the first activity I had documented in the area. Little did I know that in comparison to what was to come and what I would be allowed to film this setback was small change indeed.

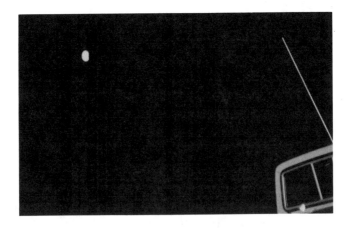

Chapter 2

The Harbor Lights

No. We do not live on a coastline, nor is there an ocean within hundreds of miles of Sedona. But in a sense we are a harbor, and as I would soon find out, these ethereal lights shine often as if to announce their arrival.

For several months my son and I noted that nightly there were many unusual lights. It is a common occurrence to walk around the ranch and spot small pinpoints of light blinking on and off. Sometimes it looks as if they are decorating the trees and bushes. At first I was fascinated with these lights but I became even more enthused when my photos came back showing luminous globes of light in various shades of color. The globes ranged from two to six feet in diameter. My eyes beheld only a fraction of their entirety. I shot roll after roll photographing these fascinating energies. Who or what were they? In time, my eyes adjusted to their presence, and occasionally I could make out a faint outline of them in their full, actual size. At no time did I sense a negativity from these lights as they floated about in a very quiet and nonthreatening atmosphere. I could almost feel them wafting lazily about, observing. The only exception might be the comet-like ones which have a more intense energy as they literally shoot into the area. They either zip through the air in front of me or they land on the ground. Even though these comet lights are more intense, I still do not perceive a negativity. In every case there is no lightning-bolt occurrence to herald their appearance, as one might expect. They merely appear and with them comes a gentle calmness.

On one very active evening I went about quickly, taking one photo after another of the lights which seemed to be everywhere. My son was out with me and we were doing our best to document all that was going on. He busily scanned with the camcorder while I pointed my camera. We shot a lot of film. Then, out of the corner of my eye, I spotted a ball of light showing through a window of the old, empty adobe homesteader's house which sits on our ranch. I stopped what I was doing instantly, recognizing the life energy emitting from that light that appeared to zoom in on us as we wandered near it. My son joined me and agreed that it was one of "them," whoever or whatever they were. Taking the opportunity, I pointed my camera in the direction of the old house and clicked, but to no avail — the batteries had instantly drained. I had just put new batteries in that day, so I knew this was not a natural occurrence. I voiced my disappointment as my son pointed his camcorder toward the culprit. He started to zoom in and . . . ZAP! His battery was also dead — and his battery had been recharged just a moment before. Obviously, that light was camera-shy. It was then that I knew for certain we would photograph only that which the strange lights allowed us to photograph.

On still another evening, while wandering about outdoors with my camera, I focused upon a small light and clicked the shutter. I had been extremely interested in its appearance, so when I turned to leave the area, my head was still turned in the direction of the light. I had gone several steps before I turned my head to the direction toward which I walked. When I did so, I found that I was in the center of a white mist which was very foglike, but was not truly a fog —

not in a normal sense, anyway. There was no fog present on that evening, nor was there any moisture in the air. There was no physical sensation such as hot, cold, wet, etc., to this foglike mass, but I instantly knew that I must get out of the fog, which is exactly what I did. Once out of the white mist, I spun around and clicked the shutter of my camera. In this photo there appeared a small window to the left. This was not visible to the eye, and there was nothing out there that night that could have emitted such a light. The area behind it was open brush country.

This next incident involving a light remains the most vivid so far in my fascinating journey of discovery. One evening I was out without my camera when, there before my eyes, a huge and brilliant light appeared in the sky above me. It was as if someone had turned on a giant TV in that dark expanse. I did not see anything but the light itself and it remained there for only a few seconds. The sight of the giant light stopped me in my tracks. Once the reality of that illumination had set in, I chastised myself severely for not having my camera with me at all times. The shot of a lifetime – and it was gone. I pondered this for several days and accepted the fact that I was evidently not supposed to document its appearance. Not then, anyway.

On another evening, as I walked with camera in hand, the light again appeared in exactly the same spot. This time it was somewhat faint, but still very discernible. I only had time to click the shutter twice, when the light instantly closed, leaving me to question whether it had been real. I stood mesmerised in that spot as I stared at the now black sky.

With high anticipation I dropped off the film, and when it was returned, again I was in for a surprise. Instead of a huge square of light in the sky, as I had expected, there before me was the scene of a place not familiar to me. (This photo and another appears in the photo section of this book under the title "About the Photograph of the Portal.") As you can see, there appears to be either a telephone pole or, as someone pointed out, possibly a ship's sailing mast in the right-hand corner of the photograph. (There are no telephone poles in this area. The nearest one is over a mile away.) In the sky a craft appears to be flying, and in the lower left-hand corner of the foreground, there is what I first thought to be a tree or bush. But Tom Dongo, upon closer scrutiny, noted that it also had the appearance of a humanoid, possibly carrying something in its arms.

This is one of the greater highlights to appear before me here. What it truly depicts, I can't say for certain at this time. Is it a window? Does it depict another dimension occupying our space? Tom Dongo's heightened psychic ability can shed a bit more light on the subject. More on that in Part Two of this book.

As you can imagine, I have asked for more opportunities. One evening I telepathically asked permission to shoot another photo of the window. Within seconds, as if in quiet response, the window flickered, and I again took a photo. With high anticipation I waited for the images to return from the lab, certain that I had again been granted a glimpse of this place depicted in the previous photo. But when I looked at the newest photo there was no open window. This time there were only balls of pink and blue light, floating down from that space to the ground. Did the window open only long enough to allow them in? Was this a special message for me to discern? It appears so. Perhaps this is saying to us that the windows are opening at this time to allow others of their type in. I believe these openings have always been on our plane and they've perhaps been the portals to allow others in, but if one were to ask my opinion of my experiences regarding this magical place, I would say that not only are they being allowed in, but they are coming in in great numbers.

I would also love to say that only compassionate beings of light are scooting through these portals, but this does not always seem to be the case. I have come face to face with a few decidedly nasty beings. I will talk about these in the following chapter.

Chapter 3

Invisibles

I have found that there are energies which definitely put my danger-sensing inner radar on alert. There are beings who walk the land yet cannot be seen with the naked eye. They will walk past and almost brush one's arm. Their footsteps can be heard, and even the grass can be heard crunching, but these beings cannot be seen. Each time I photograph them, an enormous white body of light appears on film. There is one exception to this, as we have recently discovered. After sensing a being nearby, Tom quickly lifted his camera over his head and focused on a being which was directly behind him. He did this without turning around. Tom then quickly brought the camera to his side and directed it behind him to catch the body. When the photos came back we were both somewhat surprised. There was a definite being with a head and body. Due to the angle from which the camera was directed, only the forehead and hair was visible on one photo. On the other photo there was a definite body, visible on film from the stomach on down to the ankles. These photos are provided in this book.

I am not saying that every one of these beings is negative, for I have experienced a good feeling from a portion of them. I have acquired several photos of these beings and many times there are balls of light hovering next to them. This appears somewhat conflicting because the balls of light are usually friendly. Could they be monitoring the large bodies? I don't know. At this point I can only speculate.

There is another invisible form that I have come face-to-face with. "Face-to-face" might sound illogical until I explain. One evening I heard the dogs barking frantically and fiercely out in a field. I hurried out to witness our dogs almost berserk in a frantic attack on something. The hair stood straight up on their backs and they all focused on . . . nothing. At least nothing that I could see. What, I asked myself, could get them so riled? I turned in the direction of their focus and when I did I was electrified. My solar plexus churned and I became instantly nauseous. At that moment, something approximately my height hissed loudly in my face. It was just a few feet away. My human eyes could not see it, but within myself, as Spirit, I recognized it immediately as something very negative. As far as I could see, I was alone out there with this "thing." Indeed, my protection was with me but I believe we are allowed these confrontations occasionally so that we can build our faith. I believe that from time to time we have to exercise that muscle called "knowing who you are."

In an almost automatic reflex I declared the ground holy and myself a child of God. I then demanded the creature be gone in the name of my Father. As quickly as the words left my mouth, I heard a small pop in the air nearby, and the entity was gone. At the same instant the dogs ceased and desisted in their fierce standoff, all back-hairs again lying in place. I would like to say that I pulled myself together and nonchalantly meandered back inside the house, but in honesty I must admit that my heart pounded heavily for some time. That moment was a great leap for me in the area of putting faith into action. It is a tool I would find very handy in this other-worldly arena of the unknown.

To anyone who encounters negative creatures or beings I would like to add that it is important that one declares his or her position (who one is and whom they serve) and knows this to be true. I have also used the phrase Kodoish, Kodoish, Kodoish, Adonai Tsebayoth, which is ancient Hebrew for "Holy, Holy, Holy is the Lord God of Hosts." With that I have banished the presence of those not serving the Light. As with any "dark" entities, it is good to remember that they do, and must, honor Universal Law. If one is not secure of one's position in his or her heart, it's a good idea not to play games with these beings. They can see one's light, and they don't have to obey someone who is uncertain of their own spiritual allegiance.

There is one experience that will remain etched in my memory. Even now, as I reflect back upon it, it appears almost surreal. One evening my son was entertaining a woman friend and the woman's seven year-old daughter. The three stayed in a small shell house situated on the north end of the ranch. At approximately 2:45 a.m. my son was watching out the window when he spotted what appeared to be a ship (UFO) landing nearby. He watched intently as the lights edged downward. He whispered to his friend that something interesting was taking place, and they both intently watched the development through the window. What they saw next they weren't quite prepared for.

Strolling past the window were four short-statured aliens wearing tight-fitting one-piece uniforms of a light tan color. They were what are typically called the Zeta Reticuli (also known as the Grays), only these appeared to be a bit more ashen-colored, almost white. Once the beings were out of sight and the witnesses recomposed themselves, the three of them jumped into their car and sped to the house where I was sleeping. I remember so vividly how my son vigorously shook my arm to wake me up. I can still hear the trepidation in his voice as he said, "Mom, wake up. They're here!" I raised up and said, "Who's here?" He exclaimed, "The aliens, Mom."

Needless to say, I jumped out of bed like a streak of lightning and hurried into the living room where I found the young woman and her daughter sitting in a state of shock. I quickly received a rundown of the events from my son, and then I too sat dumbfounded. Realizing it was going to be a long night, I went to the kitchen to put on some coffee. Upon returning to the living room I found the woman pointing to the front door, shouting, "There's one now!" I looked at the windows in the front door, and sure enough, I saw one of them walking past it across the small front porch. To this day I'm not certain what came over me, but I raced past the others and reached for the door. Fearing for my safety, my son grabbed me by the arm and shouted, "What are you doing?! You can't go out there!" With confidence I answered, "They can't hurt me," and, pulling free from his grip, I went on through the door and out into the yard. It was very dark.

The moment I stepped outside, the visitors became invisible. But I could still feel their intense presence and I could see a faint outline of their forms. I was incensed more than anything else at this point. How dare they intrude upon our space and then have the audacity to transform to a state in which they could see me but I could barely see them. I asked them to identify themselves. There was no response, either verbally or telepathically. I gave them another option and asked them to at least tap something three times if they were of the Light — no response. I could still make out the vague outline of their forms. I asked them to leave. They stepped back about 150 feet but did not completely leave the area. Once more I commanded their departure. They were gone.

I would have to say that I am not an expert on any of these kinds of beings, and I don't profess to know their agenda. There is a lot of conjecture on the intentions of these "Grays." Many people say they are of the "dark" or have a sinister plan for us. This may be — or it may not. I can only relate with honesty this particular experience I've had with them, and I will say that they did not leave me with a particularly good feeling.

I have learned that each instance, or encounter, must be gauged by the feelings I have at that particular time. It is easy to become overzealous with preconceived notions and allow them to direct rather than be guided by one's own inner guidance. How sad if one should have an authentic angel or being of spiritual light standing by while one commands it to leave only because it's invisible or nearly invisible. Discernment is the key here.

Things quieted down after that, but needless to say, we did not attempt to go back to sleep. Once daybreak arrived we decided to go "track" hunting. Surely these guys had left some sort of footprints, and we wanted to get them on video. The small footprints were there, all right, but we were in for yet more surprises. My son went over to a nearby fence and exclaimed, "Mom! What are those pigs doing here? See them?" He was looking through the viewfinder of the camcorder as he spoke. I turned in that direction but could see nothing unusual. I mentioned this to him, and thinking I was looking in the wrong direction, he pointed to a spot directly in front of us. "Right there!" he said. I looked: nothing. Feeling frustrated with my inability to see these pigs, he turned away from the viewfinder and was incredulous to find that what he saw through the viewfinder he could not see with his naked eye. He looked through the camera again. With frustration he added, "I tell you, they're there!" He filmed a short piece, then asked us to follow him into the house. We put the tape into the VCR, and sure enough, they were there – pigs. These were not the wild javelina that are indigenous to this area, but domestic farm-type pigs. There are no domestic pigs within 15 miles of our ranch. But there on the tape, plain as day, was a sow's head and a small piglet. Were these entities perhaps ones that had shape-shifted or was this a dimensional bleed-through? As I've mentioned, I don't have all the answers, but it sure makes for many hours of contemplation and conversation.

After witnessing the domestic pigs on tape we decided to see if anything else was showing up on film that might be invisible to our eyes. With camcorder in hand, the four of us made our way to a dry wash not far from the house. My son went in one direction and we wandered off in another, several yards away.

The next phrase to be bellowed out remains almost humorous in my memory. But at the time it was far from humorous. "Mom!" my son yelled suddenly. "There's a dinosaur in the wash!" Upon hearing that, we ran as fast as we could to join him. The seven-year-old got there much quicker than her mother and I. The little girl chimed in loudly, "Mommy! There is! There's a dinosaur!" The young mother and I arrived just in time to see what appeared to be a large tail scurrying into the brush farther down the sandy wash. The description of the creature later given by both my son and the seven-year-old girl matched exactly. It was approximately 5 feet tall, stood erect on both hind feet, and was somewhat of an earth color, or what one would call a light dusty brown.

This was time for a serious sanity check on my part. Since 3 a.m. we'd witnessed gray-skinned aliens, invisible pigs, and now a dinosaur! At the very least, I thought, I needed another cup of coffee.

I tried to gather my wits about me and then rationalized that it must surely have been a species that I had read about called the Reptilians. I mentioned this to my son and he looked at me blankly, asking, "What's a Reptilian?" I explained the belief held by many that there exists a species of humanoids from another place that closely resembles lizards. By now, this idea seemed plausible to him. But reflecting back and knowing what I know now about this fragile zone or window, I'm not so certain that what he saw wasn't a dinosaur. The only other aspect that leads me back to Reptilians is the fact that we have found, on separate occasions, large reptilian-type footprints on the ranch, and in each case it has been at a time when our animals have been harassed and terrorized by unknown and usually unseen agencies. I will explain that possibility in Chapter Four.

Chapter 4

My Frazzled Furry Friends

I have always been an animal lover and I keep many animals under my care. When some of these mysterious and unknown visitors began targeting my friends, my pets, I was more than just "put out."

One particular occurrence took place on an evening when Tom Dongo and a small group of researcher friends joined us out on the ranch. It was becoming fairly late, and up to this point we had witnessed only occasional nocturnal lights. Then, from out of the night, we heard our six horses "yelling" frantically. As we stood there, we first heard the pounding hoofbeats, then they raced past us in a highly panicked state. We hurriedly went up to them only to have them race past us again in the opposite direction. The horses were still terrorized. Obviously, something was chasing them. Something we could not see. We never did see what caused the horses to panic, for the ruckus quieted down as fast as it had started.

One day weeks later, I went out to check on the horses only to find one of them literally trapped in a tree. He was under a twenty-foot juniper and had shoved himself in there so tight he could not pull himself free of the branches. I was concerned as I gingerly pulled large branches back to free him. Other than being frightened, he was unharmed. Curious, I searched about until I found the suspected footprints nearby. These prints were approximately fifteen inches long, had three toes, and a narrow point at the heel. Nothing more happened with that incident.

Several months later we experienced some strange activity during the night. A very "heavy" feeling had engulfed the area from an unspecified energy, then later in the evening my son walked out to find his truck actually bouncing up and down! He froze in his tracks as he watched the truck not only bounce, but bend a bit in the middle. He relates that for a second or two it appeared concave at its midsection. He said the nearest thing he could relate it to was the movie *Christine*, which showed a scene of a car doing much the same thing.

He raised his camera and clicked the shutter. The resulting photo shows an incredibly intense white cloud of energy near the truck. On that same evening a photo was taken that shows a blue cloud of energy engulfing my truck as well.

I strongly suspect that the energy that caused my son's truck to bounce was related somehow to what I found the next day. Around noon I happened to be wandering about the south end of the property when I came upon one of our mares wedged into a tree. It was almost exactly like the previous incident involving the stud, only this time the horse was embedded in branches so large in diameter that I could not manipulate the limbs to allow her release. How she got in there, I will never understand. I had to go back to the house for my husband. We got a hand-saw and, between the two of us, we sawed her out of there by removing two of the big boughs. One was six inches in diameter. Had something chased her? It certainly appeared that that was the case.

That same afternoon my son came in and announced that there were more reptilian tracks by the front gate, only these had two toes instead of three. Interestingly, each time a negative energy or experience was visited upon us, we would find evidence of either the rep-

tilian or the small alien tracks. I am reluctant to draw a firm conclusion relating to all reptilian or "Gray" tracks, but up to this point
it appeared that if there were friendly ones, they weren't choosing to
grace our doorstep at this time.

Physical maladies also befell our animals during this period. Many
incidents have left our veterinarian scratching his head. The first
incident occurred with Star, one of our mares. While out one day I
noticed that her left eye appeared to be abnormally swollen, almost
bulging out of her head. The eye looked very painful, and I wondered why I had not seen the condition earlier.

After examination by the vet it was determined that the horse had
a tumor behind her eye, and based on the diagnosis, he gave us two
options. He could remove the eye and thereby attempt to remove the
tumor, but perhaps it would be best to put her to sleep, as he determined that the removal of the tumor would not give the horse very
good odds of survival.

We loved that horse very much and had a difficult time with those
two choices, so we opted for another opinion before making any dras-
tic decisions. We took her to another vet who declared that Star probably had glaucoma. He did add that this condition is extremely rare
in horses. Dogs experience this problem from time to time, but in
his words, it's almost unheard of in horses. Almost. Was this malady somehow related to the alien activity? I wondered.

We went home and considered our options. It was obvious the
horse was in pain so something had to be done. We chose to allow
our personal vet to remove the eye, and if he found a tumor behind
the eye, we authorized him to euthanize her. Our vet began the
surgery almost certain he would discover the tumor and was prepared to euthanize Star. But to his surprise, there was no tumor,
nor was there anything else which could obviously create the strange
problem.

Once the eye was removed, he took the excised organ to his lab to
dissect it for further examination. I waited outside the door as he
searched. When he stepped out to relay his findings, I noticed a very
perplexed look upon his face. "It's the darnedest thing," he said. "I
can't find any reason for the eye to swell to those extremes."

We brought Star home and nursed her through her recuperation, and I'm happy to include that she is now doing fine.

The next physical incident occurred with one of our dogs. It was similar to the horse's malady. Patches, our black-and-white dog, walked up to me one day with the biggest knot on her jaw that I had ever seen on a dog. How had that gotten there? I knew it hadn't been there the day before. When I touched the knot, it was as hard as a rock. My mind searched about for possibilities. Only two came to me: She had either been bitten by a snake or kicked by a horse. In either case I deemed it necessary to put her into the truck and take her into town for an examination.

The vet quickly eliminated snakebite and then, also, a horse kick. He probed and prodded for quite some time and deemed the lump a tumor, stating that she had probably had it for some time in order for it to be so large. I emphasized that this lump had not been there the day before, and the vet gently assured me that I had to be mistaken. No lump that massive or that hard could have grown overnight. By that time I was too frustrated to debate the confusing issue. We made an appointment to have the tumor removed three days from then and I left relieved, knowing that it was something which apparently could be remedied fairly easily. I brought Patches home and placed her in a fenced-in area.

The following morning I went out to find the tumor completely changed. It had turned soft, flattened to a great degree, and traveled over approximately 40% of the dog's jaw and the side of her face. I immediately called the vet and he, understandably, thought I might be overemphasizing the situation a bit. "But," he advised, "go ahead and bring her in for her scheduled appointment in two days." He would then look at it to determine whether the surgery would or could be performed. By the time I brought her in, this fast-moving "whatever" had now engulfed 75% of her jaw and face. I still remember the look on the vet's face when he saw her. He truly could not believe what he saw and he shook his head as he again poked and prodded this now mysterious growth. He quickly prepped her for surgery. I waited.

Once the extraction was completed he walked out. He was shaking his head again as he said, "Linda, in all my years of practice, I've never seen anything like this. The darn thing spread out and grew like wildfire, attaching to every muscle and nerve in its path. I'm sorry, but I had to remove one nerve in her face in order to get all of it out. Can you believe it? I had to go all the way to the bone. It even attached there!"

A biopsy was then performed on the mass, and no definite conclusion could be made. It was not anything really known, and yet, thankfully, it was not malignant. Patches has recovered from that episode with only one side of her mouth droopy, due to the removal of that nerve.

But unfortunately for Patches, her trials weren't over yet. Again, almost overnight, she became extremely lethargic to the point that she could barely walk. She quickly dropped from 90 to 66 pounds. She was a barely walking bag of bones. And again, I rushed her to the vet. He ran test after test while he pumped her full of antibiotics to attack whatever it was that was attacking her. No result. She continued to go downhill while he tested her for every malady known to the dog species. Finally, at a loss, he consulted with a vet in Phoenix. The x-rays and test results were reviewed, bringing the following diagnosis: valley fever. For readers not familiar with this, valley fever mainly affects humans, and it occurs in arid climates where the air can become stagnant, as in a valley. A type of fungus forms in the lungs and grows there unless it is treated for a long time with a specific medication designed to treat this disease. It is not so rare in the Phoenix area, which sits in a large desert valley. Dogs are known to get it in Phoenix. However, we live at a 4500-foot elevation and have four seasons. The ranch does sit in a valley, yet it is not so closed in that the flow of air is inhibited. Patches had never been out of this area. How did she get it?

By this time I was getting used to the perplexed look upon our vet's face. Under different circumstances it could have been very amusing. He stated that the odds of her getting valley fever were so high, he didn't care to guess what they were. There has been only one other known case of canine valley fever in the local area and that dog came from Phoenix.

The following occurrence left me wondering what was next. One quiet morning I wandered out to visit with our horses. They are scattered about the ranch, and I enjoy greeting them. I walked up to one of the mares and blinked my eyes. Was I seeing this properly? I looked again. Yes, it was true: her lovely, long golden mane was missing. The mare's mane was not cut off evenly. It looked as if it had been torn off, resulting in extremely jagged edges. Some remaining strands were barely long enough to lie down, and others were so short they stood straight up. This made no sense. These horses were basically out in the middle of nowhere. Who could have done this without our seeing it? And how could "they" have done it? Few humans have the strength to rip off big handfuls of a horse's mane. If anything, it would cut the person's hands badly.

I was still puzzling over this latest development so I walked several acres over to visit with two more of our horses. I stopped in my tracks. There was another horse with its mane torn off. What was going on? Both horses had been confined in corrals several acres from each other. It's not as if they had been in the same place at the same time to have this occur simultaneously. I did not receive any logical answers to this, and to this day it remains a mystery. But it still wasn't over. Hardly. Several days later I went out there again, and lo and behold, another horse looked extremely odd as it walked about with its forelock missing. (The forelock is the hair that grows between the ears and falls down over the horse's forehead.) Again, it was torn off rather than cut. The only different element in this instance was the fact that this horse runs free over 90 acres. Whoever was doing this obviously had no problem catching a horse. We still ask, Why? How? Who?

Another incident involving my furry friends, unlike the previous incidents, is very heartwarming and very special. There is another frequent visitor to "Galactic Park" and I will state without a doubt that she is not an animal. I call her Big Girl. This name was given in love. There is much to share about her, so I will begin with the first day I became aware of her presence. One morning we were out looking for more enigmatic footprints when my son spotted something new. There was what looked to be a human barefoot print, only it was huge. It was sixteen or seventeen inches long and close to eight inches wide at the toes. It had five toes like a human foot. It didn't take a rocket scientist to figure this one out: we now had a bigfoot around. I was a bit perplexed about this because I was under the impression that they roamed in very high-altitude country. It didn't fit (again, preconceived notions on my part). But yet, there it was right in front of us, a huge track. Could someone be playing a hoax or a joke on us, knowing that we'd been hunting strange tracks? It wasn't likely, and I reasoned that this realistic print would be difficult to duplicate.

One more piece of the puzzle: What was a bigfoot doing in a high desert, and was it friendly? I did not know much about them other than the common knowledge that they were very elusive and that most of mankind was still very skeptical of their reality. As was my habit by now, I contacted Tom Dongo. He was much more knowledgeable on some of these things than I. His years of research had enlightened him a great deal on the phenomenon. He has read all the books.

He replied that there had been in the past some local reports of bigfoot prints and it was highly probable that one was now roaming our property. We kept this in mind and added the bigfoot to our list of prints to discover. It was not long before we found many more prints, so feeling that I might be able to communicate, I left a plate of fresh vegetables out to see if it might be tempted. A friend of ours thought that they often ate roots, so I carefully chose some organic root vegetables consisting of carrots, alfalfa sprouts, and as a treat, green grapes. I used a bright red plastic plate and loaded it high with these veggies. Who knew? Maybe I could send the message that I was friendly and it would respond in kind.

There was a spot in front of the horse arena where I had found many of the tracks before, so I carefully placed the plate there and waited. Morning came and I went out to find that not only were the veggies gone, but my phantomlike visitor had left me a present. Two sticks were lying next to the empty plate, which was turned over. Was this a "Thank You"? I took it as such and began a nightly ritual of leaving the treat in the same place. The events involving Big Girl are so numerous that it would take another book to include them all, so I will summarize them and what I have learned and chronicled up to this point.

After my first couple of exchanges with the bigfoot, I went out to find messages drawn in the sand, obviously by her. How did I know it was a her? I will explain that in a moment. The first message was my introduction to her intelligence. There in the sand was the empty plate turned upside down with a perfect triangle or pyramid drawn around it. This brought a barrage of mixed emotions from me. First, it was beyond doubt that this was not an animal in the assumed sense, and I gave her due respect as such from that point forward. What was Big Girl's agenda? Did I even want to be associated with her? My feelings churned, and yet I could not turn away from her. Rather than pre-judge, I continued my attempt to contact.

In time I received many more signs and symbols. There were many pyramids or triangles, and there was even a pi sign and a little-known symbol for wavelengths between dimensions. (I had to dig deep to find the meaning of that one.) Okay. What we had here was a being who was trying to relate something to me, but what? As time went on we discovered that we could find tracks in a particular area, but no tracks leading up to or away from them. How was that? Unless she was interdimensional. Bingo. I knew I was on to something.

This discovery was reinforced later by a videotape that my son had taken one night toward the south end of the ranch. There appeared to be a great deal of activity including lights and apparent electrical energy, even to the extent that it drained the batteries of his truck and also of his camcorder. But prior to this drain he had unknowingly filmed Big Girl in etheric form. When we witnessed this on film it answered a great many of our questions about her. There, on tape, was her image, walking slowly, moving her long arms and taking giant strides. Her neck was almost nonexistent, showing a large head sitting almost on her shoulders. Had the form been more dense, it would have been exactly the being Victor saw when he was confronted by her near our arena. (More on that shortly.) Her form was so faint it was almost indiscernible, yet it was definitely there. The other enormous clue to this mystery is a UFO which also appeared on the film at the same time. Documentation in the past forty years has shown that UFO and bigfoot activity is often simultaneous. This craft is what my son was attempting to film, not realizing that Big Girl was also there at the time. The craft and Big Girl were in close proximity. At this same time a large beam of light appeared from an unknown source and encompassed the area. Was this proof that she was indeed connected with these craft? This is a possibility worth researching further in the future.

With our suspicions of her interdimensionality, we wondered what she had to do with everything else going on. In short time another aspect of her personality began to appear. I have a mare who was pregnant at the time, and I began noticing bigfoot prints in her corral. (The horse didn't seem to mind.) What was the Bigfoot doing in the corral? Obviously, she wasn't hurting the horse, so I was not really concerned, just curious more than anything else.

One evening I chose to wait up and watch from a distance to see if I could glimpse her going in with the mare. Around midnight I heard the bar of the gate bang closed! She was in there. I quietly eased down that way, but when I got to the corral she was gone. Sure enough, the following morning her footprints were there and we found her hair on the mare's pregnant belly as if she had been petting it. Somehow, I resolved, I was going to see the bigfoot – in person.

As a sidelight I will interject that at this time Tom Dongo phoned to say that a rancher a few miles from us had been having an incredibly difficult time with fetuses being removed from his mares, leaving them in a state of shock. He warned me to watch out for my mare. I instantly thought of Big Girl and wondered if she was responsible for this improper invasion on the neighboring ranch. After much thought it occurred to me that it seemed she was protecting my mare. In time this proved, to my satisfaction, to be the case. The mare has delivered a beautiful young colt, and only after it was delivered safely did Big Girl cease going into the corral nightly. She wandered in again occasionally but it was almost as if to say, "Hi." There was no longer the steady vigil.

Here is how I know this Bigfoot was female. This information was given so beautifully. One morning I went out to our "exchange" spot to find an incredible full-body print of her on the sandy ground. She had lain on her back to produce this for us. There, very visible, were the head, shoulders, elbows pointing out (she had placed her hands on her chest), torso, bottom and legs. It was similar to someone making a snow angel, only she had not moved her arms and legs. I quickly stepped off the length of the impression and deduced that she was almost nine feet tall. I called out to my husband and son and we all studied it in amazement. Then I stated emphatically that the being was pregnant. Naturally, both of them looked at me as if to say, "Now where did you get that piece of information!?" There, to the side, just above her hips, was a round bulge. Being a woman, I know that if you're pregnant you cannot rise straight up when lying on your back. You have to roll over to your side to rise. Obviously, she had needed to do this, and when she did, her protruding stomach made the oval bulge on the ground.

My husband and son skeptically said, "Okay. If you say so." In short time we found not only her footprints but, right next to them, a set of very small ones. We now had Mama and Baby. (I will note that prior to this we had also seen some prints with hers that were somewhat smaller, yet not quite baby prints. I deduced that she possibly had another child, probably adolescent size, meaning that there could be a family somewhere nearby. I have not been able to discern whether there is a male in this vicinity, but that is a possibility.) We tried to make plaster casts of the footprints, but the ground was so loose and powdery-dry that the ground simply absorbed the moisture in the plaster, leaving a useless dirt-encrusted blob.

We also determined that she is solid white. At first we found her long, white hairs near her prints, especially in her full-body print. Once, we found these same white hairs caught in the branches of the trees at least seven or eight feet high, eliminating the possibility that they could belong to any of our horses or dogs. The white is somewhat unusual in itself, as most bigfoots seen have been of the dark brown or reddish brown color. Then, in time, I found a reddish shade of hair with the baby prints, leading me to believe that it is closer to a strawberry blond color. Could they be like horses and be born with one color then shed to another in several months? I don't know. Perhaps the baby will stay red, or perhaps it will become white like its mother. In either case, it's beautiful to trace their activities. We can state emphatically that she is white because both my son and I have seen her — and Tom Dongo has samples of the hair. At approximately 2 a.m. one night my son had been wandering about near the arena when he heard something behind him. He turned to see her standing in full view. She was solid white, and her face was incredibly human, giving a very tense expression. The hair was thick upon her body and there was sparse white hair on her face. He states that even though he knew of her and her size, the enormity of her proportions still startled him. He instantly turned and ran. After going a ways he looked back to see her turning around and going back in the direction she had come from. He related that he then felt bad. Had she been trying to make contact? Had he mistaken her intentions? He feels she turned away because she did not want to frighten him. I have to agree, as I feel that she left her body print in hopes that her size would not frighten us upon an eventual meeting.

On still another occasion I was driving into the ranch at night when my headlights shined upon a clump of trees, and there above them was her head, again solid white. When the lights hit her, she ducked and disappeared quickly from sight.

I now have a very warm and loving admiration for Big Girl, as I have named her. She has been nothing but protective, and when she is near I feel very safe. We've now come to a point in our developing relationship where she will, from a safe distance, signal to me when I am outside by banging a tree or fencepost with a large stick. She will tap three times and I will respond with a tap-tap-tap. This takes place a couple of times, then I take the lead and tap four times. She responds, tap-tap-tap-tap. For now this is great for me, and I feel in time we will come face to face in mutual trust. We never carry guns, and she seems to know this.

I've learned to feel her presence, and when it is not here I miss her terribly. In relation to her signs in the sand, I've come to believe that again she is being protective by warning us of another presence, and I believe part of it is the possibility of a "base" nearby. I will be the first to say that I cannot prove this nor state it with certainty. This merely falls into the category of discernment and trusting my inner radar. The exact purpose of the base is uncertain to us at this time. But the reality of a base seems almost certain.

All in all, Big Girl is a big part of the puzzle here. If indeed she is interdimensional, this explains why she remains close to the portal. Nothing, I feel, is by accident. I believe that she is serving a function here on Earth, and as far as I'm concerned, she's more than welcome here. Perhaps the day will come when we can meet formally without any hesitation. I would like that very much.

Another part of this evolving saga includes what I call unearthly or otherworldly animals. One evening my son and his friend were driving back to our area during the late-night hours when they were forced to stop the car due to an obstruction in the road. What they saw was certainly different. There before them was an animal standing on all fours, with a shoulder height of approximately four feet. This animal appeared to be a cross between a cat and a horse. The head resembled a cat's: it was very large, with definite cat eyes, cat ears, and a cat mouth (turned down) and yet it had very long hairs all over the face. The legs were extremely long and the back appeared a bit humped. The tail was similar to a horse's tail and the body hair hung almost to the ground. It stood in the road for a moment glaring at the car. It then turned and walked slowly off into the night. What was it?

Particularly interesting is that, after this animal was seen, someone in another state reported seeing exactly the same thing. This person did not know of reports of the description my son gave.

Chapter 5

Houseguests

I use this term, houseguests, loosely because these particular guests were not invited. One evening I was sitting in the living room and looked up to see a cloud of energy hovering in the corner of the room. This was a new one. I'd seen balls of light in the house (which is not uncommon for some people) but never had I witnessed this form in the house before. Not wanting to miss the opportunity to record it, I hurried to the kitchen for my camera, which was sitting on the counter. I reached for the camera, and to my surprise and amazement, I realized that this body of energy had followed me into the kitchen and was now wrapping itself around my legs. The distinct sensation of electrical ions pricked at me. I was furious (but not angry enough to miss a good shot) so I aimed the camera directly at my legs and feet and snapped the shutter. In no uncertain terms I then told this "whatever" to leave!

When the photos were returned I found this energy form documented on film, visibly swirling about my legs and feet. It was just one more in a series of strange phenomena.

One area of phenomena that still fascinates me has to do with the sounds that filter through a thin veil that seems to be here. I will give some examples.

One quiet afternoon I was sitting in our kitchen alone. My husband was at the far end of the ranch. He had no gun with him. We live miles from anyone, so there are no city or neighborhood noises. The only thing discernible to my ears was the beautiful singing of the birds. I was enjoying this familiar serenity when all of a sudden a shot rang out and I could hear a bullet whiz past my ear. I instantly jumped, thinking someone had shot at me. I quickly looked all around, only to find nothing — no person, no bullet holes, no broken window and, much to my relief, no blood. I then sat back down and replayed the experience in my mind. I was certain the shot had gone off in the house. Later I mentioned this experience to Tom Dongo and to my family, but I decided it would be wise to say nothing to anyone else. People have been put away for less. Things were strange enough as it was.

A few weeks later, my husband and I were sitting in the kitchen having lunch when all of a sudden we heard what sounded like a huge sheet of plate glass shattering. It was as if it were right next to us, and we both jumped at the same time. I searched inside and out and could not find one piece of broken glass anywhere. I have to admit, I was a bit relieved that I was not alone this time, and was a bit more brazen than usual as I spoke of this incident. After all, this time I had a witness.

Late one evening a small group of us were wandering about the ranch investigating when the sound of chattering voices came out of the dark. They appeared to be somewhat higher-pitched than our voices and spoke in what appeared to be an unearthly language. This was not to be the only occurrence.

A few days later, at 9 a.m., I was walking through basically the same area when I again heard the same voices. I searched the area thoroughly but could find no visible sign of the source. In each instance the chattering could be heard for only a few seconds. It would abruptly start and abruptly stop.

Then, once again sitting in the kitchen, I glanced out the window to see what looked like a gray animal running outside, only this animal was a magnificent silver-gray and did not look like anything I'd ever seen before. I did not have time to make a detailed examination of it, for it was there one moment and gone the next. It disappeared before my eyes. But here's the clincher. Once it was gone, I realized I had witnessed the animal walking on thin air! It was three to four feet off the ground as it zipped along before my eyes, then it slipped into nothingness.

I find the portal both fascinating and humbling. It becomes a juggling act as one becomes aware of the "invisible mysteries" that encompass our very space, while also acknowledging the necessity to remain grounded in the obvious. I say "necessity" because many have been carried away in this knowledge and veered so far to the extremes that they can no longer function in either world. I choose to anchor myself in this realm, which is home for now, but I still realize that I am a part of all that is going on, both seen and unseen.

Chapter 6

Missing

This incident which I will relay is not mine, but my son's. Victor has given me permission to share it, that others may benefit from his experience.

One morning around 7 a.m. he left the ranch for a short hike, saying that he would be back by 9 at the latest. It was late summer and the weather was hot so he took just enough water to last a short time. He chose to take no food. Noon came, and I became concerned. He was 27 years old and certainly capable of caring for himself, but what if something had happened? I knew he did not have enough water to go much longer than two hours without becoming dehydrated. I waited. By 5 p.m. we knew something was wrong, so my husband, his son, and a friend went out on horseback to find Victor while I waited by the phone. My biggest concern was snakebite. We have four varieties of rattlesnakes here. One of these is the green Mojave — one of the deadliest snakes on Earth. If he had been bitten he would not be able to make it home, and perhaps they would not find him in time. I sent love to him, prayed, and waited for him to appear.

By 7 p.m. the sun was beginning to set. By 8 p.m. my husband and the boys returned home without him. Now what? Where could he have gone? The canyon he'd hiked to was not so large that it should be that difficult to find him. I felt somewhat put out with myself. Why had I not called Search and Rescue before it became dark? Now they would not be able to go out until morning. Okay. Time to put faith into action and wait and pray.

The clock ticked slowly as I waited for morning. Then, at 3 a.m., the phone rang. I raced to it and breathed a sigh of relief as I heard my son's voice. It was weak, and I knew that he was extremely physically stressed. "Mom, come get me." Without taking time to ask too many questions, I listened as he relayed that he was in Cottonwood, a town 15 miles south of us. This puzzled me, but I was so relieved at the sound of his voice that it didn't matter. I grabbed my keys, jumped into my truck, and sped away from the ranch. When I arrived at the convenience store he had called from I found a distressed and distraught man. He could barely walk as he limped severely on his right leg. (The cause of this injured knee will be revealed in his hypnosis, to be explained shortly.) His brand-new hiking boots had their soles worn smooth from volcanic and granite rocks. I started to ask, but when he looked at me so painfully, I told him explanations could wait till later. In reality, he didn't have any explanations yet. He wasn't sure what had happened. I brought him home and he was so exhausted he collapsed and then slept for almost two days, getting up only when necessary.

Once he had fully rested he felt he could relay what little he remembered. He had been hiking during that morning when the next thing he knew, it was night, and he found himself in the middle of unfamiliar terrain with no direction and no idea where exactly he was. He heard rattlers, so seeing the river nearby, he jumped in, knowing it would lead him to the next town — that is, if he was going in the right direction. The water was below his waist and he ended up wading and falling on slippery rocks for miles. During this time he chanced upon a camper who apparently was highly shocked to see him out there alone at night. Victor spoke to him, and the man kindly offered to share, even insisted on sharing, his camp until morning. He said he knew the area like the back of his hand. He also revealed that he knew Victor would not get out alive if he persisted upon continuing his hike during the night. Most folks would see this as a blessing and gladly accept. My son felt he could not stay there and chose to continue. He later told me he did not feel comfortable with this man and, for some reason, knew he had to get out of there. He continued on his way.

Presently he came upon a cabin and, seeing a light on, walked up to ask for help. When he knocked, a woman answered who, understandably, chose not to let him in. He asked if she had a phone and she stated that she did not. When he shared his predicament, the woman offered to loan him a warm shirt and a sleeping bag if he would bring them back the next day. He gladly agreed. (Even though the days are warm here in the summer, the nights often turn very cold. He was still wet from the river and, by now, was shivering.) This brings us to the point at which he found himself in the next town.

He shared that he had some strange memories but they were cloudy. This haunted him for a couple of days during which time I spoke to Tom Dongo, who then discussed this with a mutual friend of ours, Jim Sweet. Jim knew Dr. Carlos Warter, who is recognized worldwide as a physician/psychiatrist and author who has had experience with matters such as this. When Victor was asked if he would like help from Dr. Warter, he agreed. A session was scheduled immediately, and my son was regressed hypnotically to get to the crux of this mystery.

I need to say that there are hypnotists out there who do more of a disservice than a service. Hypnosis, especially concerning alien abduction, can be a bit faulty if one is not fully competent in this field and well versed in the area of spirituality. We had great confidence in Dr. Warter.

The regression brought out some incredible information. I will share parts of the transcript of this session, not because we wish to put on public display this very private affair, but because there is a message which, we believe, is pertinent to all of us.

In this transcript Dr. Warter will be referenced as C.W. and Victor will be referenced as V.J.

This hypnosis was conducted on July 31, 1994.

C.W. - *Go to the moment in time when you are lacking water.*

V.J. - *I see a triangle. White lights in the shape of a triangle. There is a glass or mirror. I'm going through the glass into the triangle. I'm not in the canyon. I'm inside something. I can look down and see my body below me. I see the canyon walls. I'm as high as the walls. I'm just looking. I'm now above the walls. Something is pulling me up. It's a bright light.*

C.W. - *Where are you now? What do you see?*

V.J. - *I saw something. A white oval head. There's more than one.*

C.W. - *What happened?*

V.J. - *There is a bright light. There are two lights. Two colors. One white and another color. One is right above me.*

C.W. - *Where are the oval heads?*

V.J. - *To my . . . GRAY! Gray bodies! Their bodies are gray! There's a white light behind them. A yellow light above me.*

[At this point there is a great deal of personal information, which I will go past to share the pertinent information applicable to others. I will add one additional note. It was revealed that Victor did receive an implant in his temple at the time of his abduction. When asked its function, Victor answered that it was a homing device.]

C.W. - *Where are they from?*

V.J. - *Outside of our zone. We can't see. Another dimension.*

[Dr. Warter then asked Victor to recap the events.]

V.J. - *I see a triangle. It's almost invisible form. Floating through the air. There is a bright orange light. Gray people. There is an operating table with a bright orange light above that and to the left, a white light. It is almost pulsating with them underneath it. There is a person to my right. They are holding a wand. It is gray, almost the same color as the people. This is when they do* something to my knee. I don't feel any pain, though. This person looks something like the gray ones. The wand goes into my knee.

C.W. - *Why did they select you?*

V.J. - *I believe I was in the right place. The right time. Maybe has something to do with medical, or something they're missing. I have something they need.*

C.W. - *What is their intention?*

V.J. - *Exploring without being known. To know about us. But a much higher scientific . . . almost . . . knowledge than we have.*

[At this point Dr. Warter asked Victor to use the implanted homing device to achieve answers to the following questions.]

C.W. - *Why us? Why now?*

V.J. - *Has to do with erosion on either this planet or theirs. Something is happening. I feel like they're pressured, time-wise.*

C.W. - *How long have they been happening?*

V.J. - *For a while.*

C.W. - *Do they have agreement to penetrate this planet? Do they have permission?*

V.J. - *Yes.*

C.W. - *From who?*

V.J. - *From signals they sent. Other decoys they sent into our general population.*

C.W. - *Sent to whom?*

V.J. - *The entire population. Agreement through . . . . There are more than just them. There are others too. Someone has let them into our space.*

C.W. - *Who? Is it a conscious agreement with Earth citizens or is it implanted?*

V.J. - *It's both. It's implanted, but agreement made with human beings.*

C.W. - *Consciously?*

V.J. - *Yes.*

C.W. - *Who?*

V.J. - *Head of the power.*

C.W. - *Agreement with who? What is the exchange?*
V.J. - *The exchange is protection.*
C.W. - *What kind?*
V.J. - *Galactical.*
C.W. - *For what purpose?*
V.J. - *Severe mass hysteria of . . . could be conflicts in the sky at this time which could cause planet to go into total disarray if it is brought to planet at this time. We've been bought off by keeping public . . . the public has been bought. It's secret to them. That is the deal they have made.*
C.W. - *When is the contract over?*
V.J. - *Contract is almost over. It may be over before it's over. Because problems between the two sides.*
C.W. - *Meaning?*
V.J. - *Meaning, the Government being sneaky and trying to patronize other life forms. What I'm getting at is, it's not all that rock-solid right now. There's conflict between the both sides and one is ready to break. We will be much more educated on outside life soon. Outside this planet.*
C.W. - *Good. Have you ever read or heard this information before that you're relaying?*
V.J. - *No, I have not.*
C.W. - *Is there anything else you'd like to communicate at this point in time?*
V.J. - *There's still time. There's a drop in front of me when I went back. Almost like a suction cup, but at the front of it. I'm just gliding.*
C.W. - *Go back to the point in time where you regained consciousness.*
V.J. - *I'm at Parson Springs where I was dropped. What I mean is, I wasn't really dropped. I was regained with my body.*
C.W. - *Where are you when you regain consciousness in your body?*
V.J. - *Within 30 feet of water. I refilled my water bottle and continued my hike and ran into another hiker out there.*
C.W. - *Is there any damage to your soul, psyche, consciousness or spirit?*
V.J. - *None. More aware.*

At this point Dr. Warter brought Victor out of the hypnosis. Many thanks to him for helping Victor retrieve this information. It allowed him to deal with the experience and he therefore healed within.

In reference to the information given from the Grays, please know that I am not indicating a personal declaration that all is as they stated. Were the Grays telling the truth? I don't know. If they were, it's information that serves as a warning. If they weren't, it's a great case study of their tactics. In either case, it's worth my attention.

About two weeks later my son returned home late one evening again missing approximately two to three hours. He wearily walked in and said, "I'm missing some time again. I remember something happening, but I'm not certain what it is." I immediately asked him if he again had a negative feeling, and he assured me that this was not the case. In fact, he felt incredibly positive about it, even though he didn't know what had transpired. We let it go at that and retired for the night.

The following day he stated that he would again like to be regressed if it was possible. This was arranged, and the information was illuminating. It is evident that certain answers were blocked as Victor was stopped in midsentence. This occurs during response to very pertinent questions about who "they" are, where they are from and their plans for us. These blocked answers are indicated by several dots in the transcript to show the times of hesitation.

This hypnosis was also conducted by Dr. Carlos Warter, on August 19, 1994.

C.W. - *Recall exactly the place where you left.*
V.J. - *I was at the Canyon of the Living Stone, which is . . . after Boynton Canyon. Dirt road. I stopped there. I remember figuring an arch. A figure.*
C.W. - *Arch?*
V.J. - *It's a pathway.*
C.W. - *Physical?*
V.J. - *It's a pathway into something.*
C.W. - *Just go to the moment and express it as if being there.*
V.J. - *Okay. I'm feeling something drawing me into it. I see a large*

silhouette of a person. A living stone comes to my memory as a place. They look like stones that have turned to life. There's three rocks up on top and between the three rocks through the passageway you enter into another dimension of some sort. There's a very strong energy in through there.
C.W. *- Is this while you were driving?*
V.J. *- No. I was not driving at this point.*
C.W. *- How did you get there?*
V.J. *- I had driven to this point.*
C.W. *- Why did you drive to this point specifically?*
V.J. *- I was pulled in for some reason. I pulled my car into that spot and it was a spot that was not likely for me to pull into, but I felt good. I felt I was to be given a message of some sort. The message . . .*
C.W. *- Yes?*
V.J. *- The message is . . . [long pause]. I know they have the ability to appear to . . . almost anything they want to appear as.*
C.W. *- They? Who?*
V.J. *- Meaning, light forces. It's an energy. They can do as they wish. It is good.*

[I will skip over some personal dialogue to a point where Dr. Warter and Victor are discussing a tall entity.]

C.W. *- Source. Origin. Purpose. What is its purpose?*
V.J. *- To help from mass destruction.*
C.W. *- Mass destruction of who?*
V.J. *- Of ETs.*
C.W. *- Say that again. Mass destruction . . .*
V.J. *- When I say mass destruction I mean understanding. People need to . . . there will be chaos when it comes.*
C.W. *- When it comes. What is "it"?*
V.J. *- When alien life comes to this planet.*
C.W. *- When is that?*
V.J. *- This fall. It will be before Christmas.*
C.W. *- What is going to be?*

V.J. - *Undeniable to the human race no more. Not having alien life.*
C.W. - *This probe or implant in you serves the purpose of what?*
V.J.- *Of helping prepare.*
C.W. - *Okay. Helping you prepare?*
V.J. - *Helping others and myself.*
C.W. - *Okay. Through what?*
V.J. - *Through slight amount of understanding and proof before their landing.*

[Note: In the forthcoming chapter you will find that not only did Victor indeed videotape a multitude of anomalies, but in September, following the regression, he videotaped an ET which appeared to be peeking out at him, three times.]

C.W. - *So you have a mission?*
V.J. - *Yes I do.*
C.W. - *What's the mission?*
V.J. - *The mission is to help understand. Help people understand.*
C.W. - *Is there any information that wants to come through right now? Anything you want to say specifically right now, or that needs to come forward right here and now?*
V.J. - *Don't be frightened. Be aware. You are as strong as any. We have friends from . . . [long pause]. Help. Our friends will help. They will be here to help.*
C.W. - *Who are the friends?*
V.J. - *Lots of friends. Light friends. Good friends. We have the power.*
C.W. - *We have the power?*
V.J. - *The power to override the negatives. Light and dark. There is a dark force.*
C.W. - *What's its origin?*
V.J. - *A deep evil.*
C.W. - *Deep evil? What's its purpose?*
V.J. - *Greed.*
C.W. - *How does it manifest on our planet?*
V.J. - *Through our people.*

C.W. - *Can you be specific?*

V.J. - *Scientific experiment.*

C.W. - *Scientific experiment?*

V.J. - *Yes. Of alien life and our own life.*

C.W. - *For what intention?*

V.J. - *Exploratory.*

C.W. - *What for?*

V.J. - *[No response.]*

C.W. - *What are you feeling right now?*

V.J. - *I was being watched.*

C.W. - *By?*

V.J. - *By the same being I saw in Loy Butte Canyon.*

C.W.- *Okay. Who is that being? Are you getting familiar with that being?*

V.J. - *Yes. He's always watching me.*

C.W. - *Okay, is he here right now?*

V.J. - *[Nods yes]*

C.W. - *Can you identify who that is?*

V.J. - *He's a form that I can relate to. I will be there when they will be coming. I will be one of the first to see this. I must be prepared. I will be given a message. That was the message.*

C.W. - *Good. So you're definitely no victim at all?*

V.J. - *No.*

[Jim Sweet was videotaping the session and, at this point, asked Victor a question.]

J.S. - *Are the Grays the good guys or the bad guys or both?*

V.J. - *The Grays are neutral at this point. The Grays play games. They don't . . . . We don't . . . . They are not . . .*

J.S. - *Why do you think the Grays are coming around so much?*

V.J. - *I believe that there are many . . . I know that there are many different forms of life beings on this area at this time. The Grays are territorial. They wish to have territorial achievement if you let them have it.*

C.W. - *Good. You mentioned the Golden Ones?*

V.J. - *They are of the light. I see three of them. I see choice . . . three choice ones.*

C.W. - *Can you describe their hair?*
V.J. - *They are of a luminous gold, beautiful head, figure not like that of the Grays, or of any that I have seen. Their bodies are short, they're slightly wide, their arms are long and can move flowingly. Their bottom half does not have a defined form.*
C.W. - *Would you say that's similar to angels described in other times?*
V.J. - *Yes. Absolutely. They can throw the light with their hands.*
C.W. - *Can they mobilize themselves without ships?*
V.J. - *Can you say that again?*
C.W. - *How do they journey?*
V.J. - *They journey as light. They can journey up to three at a time in a small vessel, which is actually a light.*
C.W. - *What's the outcome of this process? Go through that probe to the time when the outcome has played itself out and, if you are willing, describe what you see.*
V.J. - *I see people being drawn. They are helped and flown up . . . off. Being escorted as . . . by super angels. Up.*

[Dr. Warter then brings Victor out of the hypnosis.]

Since that time Victor has been allowed to videotape some of the most incredible footage of UFOs, alien life forms, invisibles, and other phenomena. It is astounding what he has been given. He is presently putting this footage in a form to be commercially available sometime in the future.

Chapter 7

Harassment

A t this juncture I will describe another suspected, possibly temporary, facility, near our ranch. We suspect this to be military due
to the abundance of black helicopters flying into the subject area. My
son, Victor, was hiking through this particular canyon when he came
upon a facility which was not known by any of the locals to be there.
He found it extremely interesting and, with the camcorder, proceed-
ed to zoom in on it and film. What he found is pretty incriminating
in my opinion. Lined to the left of a large compound there was a caravan of all-white vehicles. These vehicles included what appeared to
be a large box truck with the back door lifted up; a pickup truck; a
4-wheel-drive Blazer-type vehicle; and a couple of smaller trucks.
Then, closest to the two huge open doors of the facility was a white
18-wheeler, backed in to unload (or having just loaded) what appeared

to be a massive craft. It was an airborne type of vehicle but it had no wings. It was oblong, with two large windows in the cockpit section, and the remainder was extremely sleek.

Walking about the area were five men all dressed in solid-white coveralls. What was going on there? Feeling very nervous, my son continued to film until he "felt" someone looking at him from behind. He slowly turned and saw something he could hardly believe. There, in a bush, was a small alien-type being rising up to look at him. It peeked out of the bush a couple of times before Victor overcame his amazement and turned the camera on the being. Almost as if posing for him, it peeked out three more times and is now recorded on film.

Intruding upon this mystical experience, my son heard the sound of a jeep roaring up toward his vantage point, over rough terrain. At the same time a plane flew over him very low. The plane appeared to be photographing him. He quickly raised the camera to film the plane for a few seconds then raced out of the area. He hid in the desert until they gave up the search. On film it is clear that a bright flash emanates from the plane, but one would reason that they could take a photo without using such a brilliant flash of light. The flash is extremely large and, when shown slowly, frame by frame, almost engulfs the entire plane. Again, what was going on? We would certainly like to know.

On another occasion while he was hiking near the ranch, the same type of plane flew over and it too flashed. This time a brilliant red light completely consumed the entire camera lens and all filming ceased. It appeared that the camera was dropped. Victor had no recollection of this incident and only dimly remembered it when he saw it on film.

There are additional instances which, I believe, may be related to these bases.

For the past two years we have been witnessing the appearance of black, unmarked helicopters flying extremely low over our ranch. The crafts come in so low that the roar of the blades sways our trees and scares our animals. On two occasions we have seen missiles attached to the crafts as if they were prepared for a fight. Along with this provocative activity there is a huge cargo plane that has also buzzed the ranch so low that everything in our house rattled. The plane was large enough to carry a military tank inside of it. It would fly so low that it had to lift its nose to clear a tree above the house. Once past the ranch it would circle around and head toward the area of the suspected secret military base. First of all, it is illegal for these huge, fixed-wing aircraft to fly so low. Secondly, what is a plane of that size doing in our area? It buzzes our home then flies into an area where there supposedly is nothing. Certainly nothing that could accommodate a plane that size.

There are also ongoing appearances of white vehicles in the area. Many times they are without license plates, and the men in every case look like military personnel. Last summer, 1994, in the early morning hours, a large white caravan was seen by campers heading down the dirt road past our ranch into a canyon where, supposedly, there is nothing. Yet another time, at night, my son saw a large caravan in the same vicinity, only this time the vehicles were yellow and had not a spot of dirt on them. They shined immaculately, and there was an official-looking insignia on each of the doors. Due to the darkness my son could not read what the insignias said. He said that he was behind the caravan, and when they saw him, they all pulled over to allow him to pass. He states that it seemed like an attempt to get rid of him so that he would not follow. Local residents have agreed that there was no reason for trucks that big to be out there, especially at night.

I am aware of the speculation by many in the U.S. that the white vehicles belong to the United Nations, a suspected faction of the New World Order. This may be true. I, personally, cannot state this to be a fact, but speaking from my own experiences I can state that something secretive is obviously going on. The continuing appearance of these vehicles has certainly demanded my attention, but the fact that my family has now been involved has greatly irritated me.

We have a young man working for us who has become very much like family. He is at our home as much as our own children are and we've pretty much taken him into the family fold. It is easy to see how someone might mistake him for one of our boys, since he is within their age range. One evening he was walking down the main street in Sedona after dark when a white van pulled up in front of him and stopped. There were four men in the van and they "kindly" offered him a ride. He said, "Thanks, but I'm just going another block or so." He attempted to continue on his way when one of the men reached out and grabbed for him, ordering him in a threatening manner, "We said get in!" The young man then spun around to avoid being seized and took off in a dead run in another direction. The white van did not try to follow him.

On another evening one of our sons, John, was driving cab fares for another son, Bobby, who owns a taxi service in town. At 1 a.m. he received a call to pick up two fares at a restaurant in Sedona. The destination of both passengers was Cottonwood. One of them was to be taken to the airport; this man was in no hurry so he suggested that they drop off the man in town first. John did as requested. During this time it was noted by all three that a silver car had followed them the entire way from Sedona to Cottonwood. This car had left the restaurant at the same time as our son's van. On the way, one of the fares asked our son if he knew they were being followed. He answered yes and said that he had been watching them.

Upon reaching their destination in Cottonwood, those in John's van noted that the silver car had not only followed them, but had stopped when they did. It then did a U-turn in the street so that it could continue to follow them. By this time our son was definitely on alert and waiting to see what was going to happen. With their stalker still on their heels they headed up the long road to the airport. It was becoming quite evident that they were being tailed. Why? Who? The silver car sped up, passed them, then spun around in the street so that it was facing them from the opposite direction. It then started flashing its headlights. The airport passenger became extremely nervous, ordering our son to stop immediately, stating that he was certain the car following them was the police. Our son inquired why he thought this and asked the passenger if someone was after him. After assuring our son that he had done nothing wrong, the passenger remembered that the man driving the silver car had gotten out of a white van in the restaurant parking lot in Sedona and then entered the silver car. In the white van were several men in uniforms. Alarm systems went off in our son's head. What would he do?

There wasn't much time for planning or even thinking as the silver car speeded up and pulled alongside them, very close to the van. Their windows were now facing each other. In an instant the driver darted out of the silver car and was at our son's window, demanding of him what he was doing out this late at night. Our son answered that it was really none of his damn business, but if the man had to know, he was driving a cab and delivering this fare to the airport. Then, in return, our son demanded the identity of this stranger. The man, whose appearance and accent seemed Hispanic, stood there in his slick Armani-style suit. He mumbled something about being with the local police department, but he could produce no badge. Our son asked to see the man's ID, and the stranger acted as if he did not hear, demanding again to see our son's driver's license. Again, our son asked to see his badge. None was brought forth.

The accosting stranger was getting increasingly riled and our son was growing no less agitated. Our son finally told the stranger that he thought he was full of shit. He was no cop! Hearing this, the man turned toward his car to reach for something on his dashboard. In the dark, it appeared to our son that it might be a gun and, fearing for both his safety and that of the fares, he reached out and grabbed the man by the collar with one hand. Normally this would be difficult, but our son is 6-foot-3, 240 pounds, and an award-winning arm wrestler. He has terrific strength in his arms.

Before the man could react, our son had lifted him into the air, arms and legs flailing, and pinned him to the side of the van. The fare began to panic, asking what my son thought he was doing. Was he nuts or what? Our son told him he'd had to do this or risk getting shot. Still holding the man to the side of the van, my son accelerated until he got to about 40 mph. He then literally tossed the man out onto the road. The man rolled a number of times and, I was told, bounced several times. Hearing this, my heart sank as I wondered what happened next. Was the man killed? Our son assured me that he slowed down long enough to see that the man got back to his feet (after falling down twice) then began making his way to the silver car. He apparently was a bit battered, but functioning.

My comments on this? First of all, if this was a real police officer, why did he not present his badge and ID upon approach of our son, as all plainclothes police are required to do? And, if it was the police, why was there not a police report or an assault warrant put out for our son? Even if they did not know our son's name, they knew the name of the taxi service. It would be very easy in a small town like this to find him. To this day, nothing has been said or done about the incident. Who was this man? Who did he really work for? The "terrified" fare was taken to the airport, which, oddly, was closed. He told our son that he had a scheduled flight at that hour. Was he really a fare — or was he a lure to get our son in a secluded area at that late hour?

Many things come to mind, but I would like to share my personal thoughts on this. Firstly, these harassments were not performed by official local policemen. Secondly, if they really wanted our sons, they could have taken them. This was obviously a case of harassment. Next comes the question of why? Could it be because our son Victor has a tape of a facility which supposedly does not exist? Not only does he have the tape, but it shows ETs and suspicious aircraft. With all this taken into consideration it would appear that there is reason to suspect some shady dealing on behalf of this group. Government, perhaps?

One last statement on this issue. One evening I too was followed from town, at 11 p.m. after a meeting where I showed this same film to a group of local researchers. I discovered that a white car had followed me from the researcher's residence. I wondered what to do. We live twelve miles from town; eight miles of it is desolate dirt road where only a few other families reside. This vehicle was out of place here, especially this late at night. The car came closer and closer. Something was obviously wrong. I accelerated my truck past 40 mph. This relatively slow speed is nevertheless extremely dangerous for anyone not familiar with the rough, winding dirt road. The car stayed with me. I looked at Victor's tape next to me on the seat and suspected that it could have something to do with this. Realizing my options were limited, I shouted out in desperation, "Jesus, help me!" I looked up into the rear-view mirror and — the car was gone. It had stopped almost instantly in the middle of the road, lights off, motor stalled. I slowed and looked back again. Yes, sure enough, the car was stalled in the road. I prayed a grateful "Thank you" and raced on toward the ranch.

It appears that that night my protection was on alert and functioning. What is going on out here that must be so secretive? Why (as it appears) are "they" so threatened? I believe there are some things which we are discovering (and sharing) which they do not wish to be disclosed. I speak only from personal experiences and conjecture, but I feel the true agenda is still much more complex than I have mentioned. Believe me when I say that we are not the only ones to come face-to-face with these secretive elements. Stories such as this and much worse have surfaced in recent years.

It would be easy to become militant on this issue and "prepare for battle." I don't aspire to that perspective. I know that whatever they are creating is something that will ultimately come back upon them. It always does: one cannot escape that truth. I will continue to go forth in my endeavor to enlighten whoever wishes to know what I, personally, have experienced.

Chapter 8

Ministering Spirits?

There are so many incredibly beautiful things that have occurred and still are occurring. It's easy to get caught up in the more negative aspects of this phenomenon. In reality, the good far outweighs the "not so good." As I've mentioned, some of the beings or life forms which frequent this place are very peaceful. When one is near them, a cloak of serenity appears to cover the entire area. It's almost as if time stands still and I find myself absorbing the love which permeates all space about them. I will relate a couple of instances of this.

One evening Victor was asleep on the sofa and awoke to find a tall ethereal form coming from the hallway that leads to the master bedroom. The tall form was somewhat luminous and wore a long blue robe. To this day my son says this being emanated the greatest love he has ever experienced in his lifetime. He related that it was a love totally different from what we, as humans, normally express to each other.

While he lay there wide awake in amazement, this being expressed to him telepathically that my son should not be afraid, for he was in no danger. The beautiful being then expressed that it knew us and visited often. (My son related that he could not remember exact words but the impression was definitely implanted in his mind.) Victor said he was left with the impression that it loved us very much, which is not surprising due to the apparent capacity it had for love. The message was then given to my son that he would not need to learn anything from others, for he would be taught what he needed by this being. I believe the message was, "We will teach you." The glowing entity then crossed the living room and floated through a wall while my son watched.

After Victor witnessed this, he jumped up and threw back the drapes which covered the window above the sofa. Outside, in addition to the tall being, he saw a smaller one beside my truck. It turned to look at Victor and telepathically requested that he follow. The being then lifted one knee, wrapped its arms about the uplifted knee, ducked its head and transformed into a ball of light which then disappeared. Perhaps these are the balls of light we see so often, and if they are, this would explain why we experience such peace when they are near.

I do know that there are some who will jump to the opinion that these beings are evil and deceiving. I am well aware of the teachings and theories of many religions. My purpose in this message is to relate exactly what is occurring and what I, personally, have experienced without any influence from established doctrines. Many will cling to a preconceived doctrine and then take all life experiences and mold them to fit into this structure. I choose to take life in its purest form and give merit to each experience individually. These beings were peaceful and beautiful to my son. They emitted a goodness from within, and were accepted that way. This is not to say that other beings much like them will not appear and give a completely different impression. If this should occur, then that experience will be intuitively classified as such. Yes, there are beings who will come in a disguised light who might perhaps deceive many, but if one is functioning from within, one will be able to discern these imposters. Preconceived notions take away our ability to discern with clarity.

I believe the reason we as humans have the need to place everything into preconceived categories is that we are fearful of trusting our own judgment. If we follow what someone else says the experience should be, we are then relieved of the responsibility of making personal choices. I know the teachings of the Bible, the Eastern teachings, and much of the other received wisdom. I personally see truth in them when they are accepted with a pure heart. Please do not misinterpret as negative my comments on religions and doctrine but I feel humanity's own interpretations and their need to categorize all, within their limited understanding, have tarnished the original messages. Real truths are written from beyond man's limitation. In many instances, it is an individual we listen to when learning of their meanings, and that person learned from another, who learned from another, etc. Perhaps we should allow ourselves, as spirit from within, to perceive the true messages.

One morning I awoke at 3:50 a.m. It was very dark, but rather than go back to sleep, I got the distinct impression that I should look out the window of the bedroom door that leads outside. I peeked out and saw a white mass near the horse's water troughs, which are located just left of our water-holding tank. I blinked and looked again. Sure enough, it was white, and this mass of light was approximately my height. I measured its height by noting that it was perhaps two feet higher than the split-rail fence posts. I noticed that this form moved fluidly and first appeared to be an indistinct mass, then took some form. It turned slowly, and I saw what appeared to be arms extended out a bit. It then bent over at the waist and appeared to do something on the ground. It then rose again and repeated this process a number of times while I watched. In the period of almost an hour during which I watched it, it changed form, from a ghostly mass to an ill-defined body, to a big ball of light, back to a body, and then back to a mass. It was very wispy yet at times became more dense. Three times while I watched, a ball of light appeared right in the middle of its form then disappeared. This small light fluctuated from red to green to white, and the whole time that I viewed this process, balls and pinpoints of light appeared and remained close to it. At one point a ball of light appeared directly in front of my window, and I got the distinct impression that it was watching me. It then disappeared quickly. Next I saw a comet-like streak of light shoot straight through the air not far from the white form, perhaps four feet above the ground.

The white form occasionally flickered like a fluorescent bulb does, and when it did this, it became less dense; it was then that I could see almost tubular forms within the outer form. One time while it flickered I also saw three tubular forms with a ball of light above them. When it stopped flickering it once again obtained an almost human, yet cloud-like, form. Above its head I saw an electrical arc such as you see when you're photographing electricity. Then, shortly after that, above its head appeared a tubular light. It was magnificent.

Also, while watching this, I spotted a craft approaching from the north. It was definitely not the aircraft normally used here on Earth, for it moved extremely slow, finding its way to the hill on the west side of the ranch then slowly lowering itself below the hill as if landing. I've watched them do this before, but the unique thing about this one was that just before it dipped below the horizon it emitted an incredible halo of light all around it, which then seemed to draw itself back into the craft. It looked like pictures one sees of sunbursts. I distinctly remember seeing spikes of light which looked almost silver. It all happened very quickly.

I thought of going outside with my camera, but I knew the form would disappear if I made a noise going out. Also, I knew it would sense me even if I was quiet. From my vantage point at the window, there was a tree slightly in the way, and the angle would have made videotaping quite difficult. I had to watch from an angle, which made my neck a bit stiff. Taking all into consideration, I thought it better to watch the form with my eyes and record the information mentally rather than risk scaring it off.

I will say emphatically that I was not asleep and this was not a dream. In fact, during the process of this, I hurried in to wake my son so that he could witness the form also. He was extremely tired and did not rise easily, so I chose to let him sleep.

What was it? I don't know. Perhaps a hologram? Perhaps a life form? Whatever it was, it was fascinating to witness.

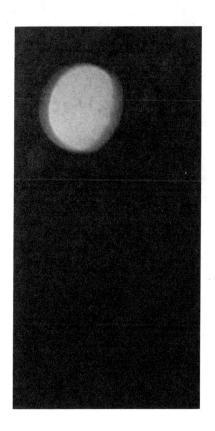

A Few Last Thoughts

The known is finite, the unknown infinite; intellectually we
stand on an islet in the midst of an illimitable ocean of inex-
plicability. Our business in every generation is to reclaim a
little more land.

— *Thomas H. Huxley*

Now that we have this information and evidence, what shall we do
with it? Being human, we need to classify or categorize. I will
share my perspective on this.

There are many facets of this world in which we live. Some visible, and this we accept without question. We see it, feel it, hear it,
smell it, and therefore it is real. But what about the things that go
beyond these senses and yet are surely as real as what we can experience outwardly? I speak of these things with certainty only because
I can relate to them on a first-person basis of authenticity in my life.
I have watched beings go from visible to invisible and vice versa. I
have "felt" invisible life forms brush past me. I have even felt and
heard some hiss loudly in my face. I have felt a presence not seen by
my eyes, yet when photographed it became real and visible. I have
heard noises and voices, yet could not see the bodies attached to the
sounds. I have peered into what appears to be another dimension not

normally seen by those here on Earth. Why is this? Why now? Could it be that the time has come when this invisible world is due to be revealed?

Throughout time there has always been a small handful of the population who have the privilege of viewing this unseen world through their own eyes. The invisible element of our dimension has always been here. But what about now? I do not have that heightened psychic ability that Tom and some of the more famous seers in the past have. Yes, I am psychic to a degree, but for the most part, the greatest images shown to me have emerged on film. This tells me that not only was I supposed to witness them, but I believe I was given lasting images on film in order to share them with others. Perhaps it is time for all of those who wish to see, to do so.

Who are these visitors? Where do they come from? What do they have to do with us? Again, conjecture runs rampant on these issues, and I do not wish to redundantly repeat all of the theories. Instead, I will share my innermost feelings on the subject.

No favorites are being played at this time in relation to who gets to come in. I have stood near the portal and felt every energy possible as they come in and wander about. As I stated a time or two when in the midst of their company, "How dare they come in like they own the place!" But in reality, do we really own this place? I doubt it. Like them, we are merely passing through. Earth is a wonderful element for those of us who need to be "purified by fire." In other words, if we can get out of here spiritually intact, then we've come a long way. It's time for bigger and better things. I believe that this surge of "company" upon our plane can be a great tool for mustering that muscle I spoke of earlier: knowing who you are.

But let us not forget the beautiful, loving beings who are also in our midst. Angels? Maybe. There are incredible beings who are here to assist us in this leap of realization. We are truly not alone in our journey. But are they real? It certainly appears so as I stand out there, tingling from their energy. Could they merely be what I have termed "tools" to advance our awareness of our true selves? Optical illusions could be brought forth as explanation, until I recall Big Girl tapping out her cryptic "Hello" for me. This brings me full-circle to realize within my own understanding that they are real but within a different level of parameters than what we gauge by here on Earth, in the dimension that we reside in. I believe that we are sharing a space-time continuum, and it is now that these dimensions are merging to place another piece in this puzzle we call life. As these pieces are put into place, the fuller picture comes into view.

Now comes the issue of perception. There are many ways one could look at this, and in general, the major population might see a very negative aspect and react in kind. This is understandable. Also, do we wish to know that we are being watched by invisibles? Do we want the responsibility of discerning their agenda? What are their plans for us? And what will we do if we see them and they don't look at all like us? Our lives are comfortable as they are. Does this mean that everything we thought was, is not? Quite a scenario for creating a paranoid population, is it not?

What then can we do to alleviate or rectify this? Perhaps an altering of our perceptions will be of assistance in this matter. Sure, we can be watched. And once we realize we have the ability to watch them also, what a great chance to break free from the illusory constraints we've been bound to. What a great chance to peek into another aspect of this world of which we have been ignorant, though it is still as real as what we've known here. (Only at this point could we communicate, for the majority of them will not impose upon us in that manner.) If there is fear of this communication, it cannot take place.

Yes, it would be great to take the responsibility of discerning their agenda, or more aptly put, whom they serve. How freeing it would be to make this determination without consulting a person or a book. How liberating to just reach within for that wisdom and knowledge. And along with that would be the assurance of our rightful position in this cosmos, which would give us that instant ability to cast off any undesirables without being crippled by fear.

Their plans for us have no place in our lives. Only we can choose which course our lives will take, and it is our confrontation with both the light and the dark which will ultimately bring us to this conclusion as we recognize our true power – again, freed from a bondage.

What if they don't look like us? (Trust me: some do and some don't.)

So what? I'm sure if we looked at ourselves in an objective manner, we would realize that we look pretty strange to them. Again, so what? What is the outer shell? Merely a convenient vehicle to hold us as spirit and get us about. These bodies are only temporary and are far from our true form, as theirs are. We are all spirit in our true sense and we return to that when we leave here. This forces us to go past the outer and look toward the inner, which is again a form of discerning.

Does this mean that everything we thought was is not? No. It means that everything we thought was is only a tiny fraction of the whole picture. We don't have to throw in the towel and declare our existence a sham. It's truth and it's what we've needed at the time. But as in toddling children, perhaps we can be allowed to wander out of our small, confined area to see some more of that great world out there. By doing this we can see another aspect of ourselves that we weren't previously aware of. Each of us is an extremely important part of everything that goes on, both here on Earth and elsewhere.

And lastly, who are they and where do they come from? They are nothing more than created beings, the same as us. Period. Their agenda is another story. Every being has free will, and like us, some of them make some very poor choices resulting in harm or damage to another being. Check these guys out before inviting them in for coffee.

Where they come from is, simply stated, the same place we came from. There are multitudes of places in this universe that we all traverse on our journeys, and many planes and dimensions we temporarily call home. I call it musical planes. We go from one level to another, passing each other along the way, each struggling to return to our true home. I choose to bow to all on this path, whether they be reacting as light or dark. This does not mean that I am chummy with a being who will hiss at me or attempt to undermine my lineage of God, but I do honor their struggle. I believe it is only through this understanding and love of our brotherhood that we can grow. Again, I am not advocating their negative attacks; rather, I am seeing their true existence prior to any altered paths they may have chosen. Or could it be that they are, as I stated earlier, performing the function of assisting us in our growth? Either way, it is only through our confrontations and, ultimately, the passage through them, that we can advance. If we stand frozen in fear we will be denying our true position.

Like many, I have wondered out loud what home was like and I even became homesick for a time. Why couldn't I be allowed to recall my true home? But as Spirit so gently assured me, "How you would dislike silver if all you could remember was gold." That's good enough for me. I know that home is gold. It is far better than the silver we have here, and yet, how great this place is, for it prepares us for home. All is within, waiting to be claimed. There is nothing to seek outwardly, only something to claim. When we come to this realization, we will be instantaneously transported to that Eden.

I pray that the information I have shared with you is taken in a positive perspective and will be used as a stepping stone rather than a stumbling block. May your life's journey flow forth in God's Love and Light.

About the Photograph
of the Portal

We were going to include this photograph along with the others until we began to notice some aspects of it that are highly unusual. So we decided to present it in a section of its own. We offer no explanation for this photograph. We have no idea how it happened to appear on two successive prints. Linda was looking in the direction of the third portal when she noticed a light appear in the area of the portal. She snapped two quick photos while the unusual light was visible, and the following is the result.

The scene, or TV-screenlike picture, is about fifteen feet off the ground, judging by the outline of a thirty-foot-tall juniper tree just to the right of the screenlike depiction in the center of the photo.

The two photographs are not identical and show movement of

objects between one shot and the other. Also, the nearest telephone pole is over one mile from where the photos were taken. Both photos were taken in an arid and brushy desert, but the scene depicted seems to indicate an oceanside scene or that of a late afternoon sunset on a sloping plain.

Upon close inspection, one sees some nearly hidden objects in the photos. In both photos are pyramids — two in the first photo and three in the second. There is what appears to be a flying bat in the photos, along with what looks like the number 39 with a large dot directly after the 9. Some who look at the photo claim to see a 39 and an N, not a 39 with a dot. Personally, I can clearly see a 39 with a dot.

Then there is the UFO. It is a perfect disk shape with a rounded dome on the top. With the way the sun shines on the telephone poles and the UFO, the time looks to be between 2 p.m. and sunset on a clear day.

In the lower left-hand corner is the most intriguing object in the photos. It appears to be a humanoid in a space-type suit, and the humanoid seems to be carrying something in its left arm that looks long and thick and somewhat U-shaped. The right arm seems to be raised and pushing forward as if the humanoid is reaching for something with its right hand. The shoulder pad or suit hinge on the right shoulder is pushed upward in the photo in a way that is consistent with the right arm being indeed extended. The right hand can be clearly seen in the original photo. The humanoid is looking to the left as if watching something or someone, while it reaches out with the right hand.

In the first photo it appears that the humanoid's head is facing directly toward the camera and its right arm seems to be raised higher than in the second photo. There may be a second humanoid to the right and slightly behind the first, or front, humanoid. However, there is too little detail to be certain of that. There is an object near the telephone pole that has dropped from sight in the second photo. Perhaps at some time, computer enhancement can be performed on these two photos to bring out the objects with far greater clarity.

Was this scene presented intentionally by some cosmic source as a great puzzle — like the crop circles — for us to decipher and interpret? Is there a clear message hidden in the photo? Does it all relate somehow to the time and place the photograph was taken near the Loy Butte/third portal area? We wish we had the answers.

There might be a partial answer to at least a part of the puzzle. It's the pyramid in the upper-left of both photos. In James Hurtak's now classic book, *The Keys Of Enoch*, there is a remarkably similar photograph along with an explanation from Hurtak. The photo in *The Keys Of Enoch* was taken by the Mariner 9 Mars Probe on February 8, 1992. These are segments of the explanation of the Mars pyramids from *The Keys Of Enoch.*

> Enoch explained how the Brotherhood of Light established pyramids on certain planets in this solar system in relationship to Saturn the key to the planetary table and density levels of other forms of intelligence operating within our solar system. These pyramids are built in grid formation and are connected to chronomonitors which measure the vibratory levels of consciousness on a given planet in units of a thousand years. They determine when successive consciousness worlds can accept physical extraterrestrial guides which nurture God level zero (0) growth to God level one (1) status, thus completing the pyramids at God level one (1) status.

In another section Hurtak continues along this line.

> Human intelligence must be initiated into the pyramidal functions of Light before they can be advanced to the next ordering of evolution, the next consciousness time cell. Man will then see he is co-citizen and co-participant of star kingdoms which are part of a cosmic pyramid, which is surrounded by a crystalline sphere separating this universe from other universes.

— Tom Dongo

Actual photograph showing scene from the portal with the tall
juniper tree to the right.
(The tree is not visible in the book reproduction.)
This is Photo #2.

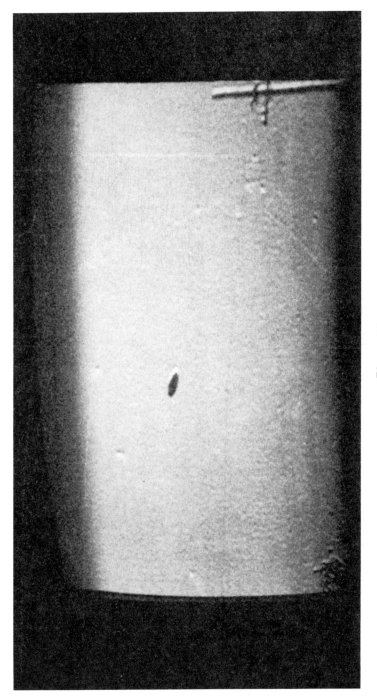

Photo #1

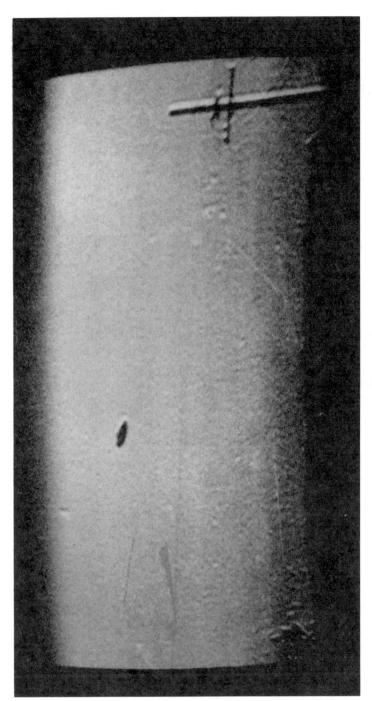

Photo #2

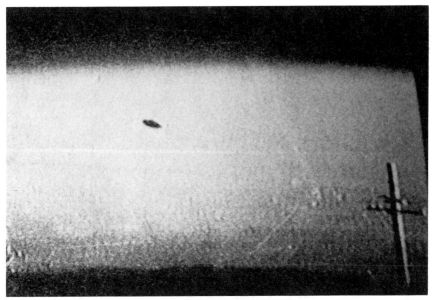

Photo #2

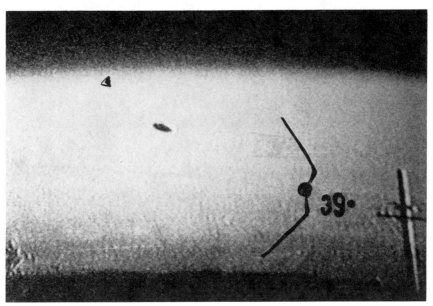

Photo #2 with the bat, the pyramid and the number 39 highlighted.

From photo number one.

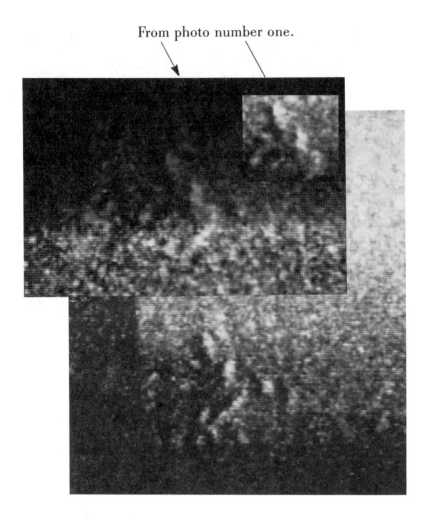

400% Enlargement of lower left portion of photo #2
showing "humanoid."

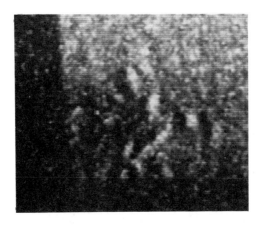

These images are from photo number two.

Helmet with ridge over eyes.
(Eyes and mouth discernible.)
Face toward camera.

Shoulder pad

U-shaped object
under left arm.

Shoulder pad
and left arm
holding object.

Right hand
reaching down.

Left knee with
flexible joint
in suit.

Right knee with
flexible joint in suit.

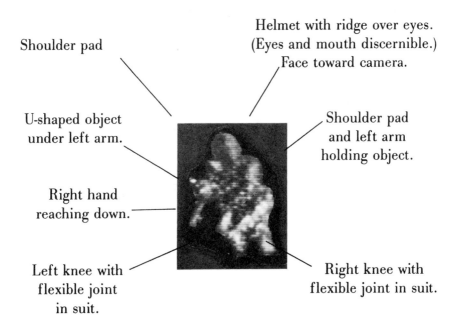

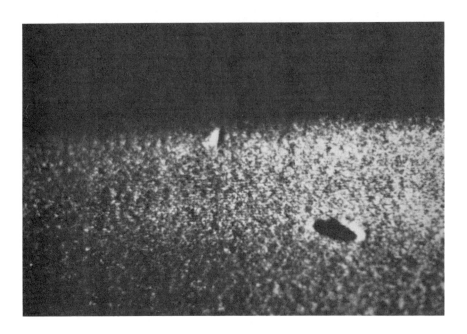

Enlargement of pyramid on photo #1.

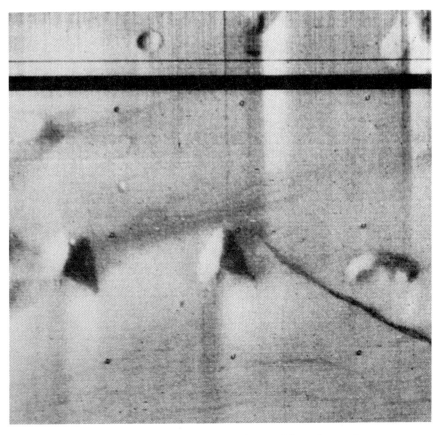

Reproduction of the pyramids on Mars from the
NASA Mariner 9 Space Probe.

PART TWO
by Tom Dongo

Chapter 1

The Portals in Sedona

After ten years of almost full-time UFO and paranormal research here in Sedona I have come to the conclusion that, along with the world-famous energy vortexes, there are also interdimensional portals in this area. These portals, or windows, seem to be entry and exit points into another dimension or universe or place that we, at this point, do not fully understand. This sort of thing isn't happening only in Sedona. Around the world there are a number of these anomalies developing or, perhaps better put, just being discovered. My estimate would be that there are probably hundreds of these portal-type anomalies spread around the globe.

UFO and other paranormal activity often is clustered in specific areas, and after a time the attention of researchers is unavoidably and irresistibly drawn to these areas. Crafts and other strange flying objects are seen and photographed far more frequently in these usually small zones. Unknown objects are often seen suddenly appearing or disappearing in and out of these mysterious zones. The logical conclusion is that these anomalies are entry and exit points for these travelers or objects from who knows where. Many of these anomalous zones around the world are located in regions of high magnetic or electromagnetic activity. Sedona, with its red rocks full of iron particles, is certainly one of those magnetic regions.

In the Sedona area indications are that there are several minor portals. One is near Rachel's Point in Long Canyon. Another is near the top of Schnebly Hill, and two or more others are in Boynton Canyon. In the Sedona area we also seem to have three primary, or major, portals. One is in the general tract between Bell Rock and Verde Valley School, an area of about ten square miles. Another portal is near the top of Secret Mountain, adjacent to the mouth of nearby Secret Canyon. This comprises an area of about two square miles. The Secret Mountain portal has been inactive for at least nine months. I think this portal was intentionally destroyed; I'll go into that later.

The third primary portal is between Red Canyon and Loy Butte, an area of approximately three square miles. Due to the presently small amount of human habitation in the Red Canyon/Loy Butte area (it's mostly in the Coconino National Forest) we have been able to concentrate study there without being bothered or distracted. We have precisely located the third portal – we know exactly where it is. It's not easy to locate one of these anomalies precisely. It takes years of trial-and-error observation. This third portal's actual size is quite small. It measures approximately thirty feet in height and one hundred feet in length and width. Because of the extreme vulnerability and, we think, fragility of this portal, our research group has agreed to not openly publicize the exact location of this particular portal. Humanity often tends to overrun and ultimately destroy things of natural or esoteric value. At this time we need to avoid that sort of possibility until we can study this mysterious zone in greater depth. "In greater depth" means any electronic, magnetic, photographic or psychic means we can employ that won't harm, alter or destroy this portal anomaly.

We know little about this third portal. We do not know how sturdy, or how fragile, it is. These anomalies in other parts of the world have indeed been known to vanish if too much human pressure is focused on them. This is obvious from similar activities, elsewhere, in the past. Sometimes it also seems that these types of anomalies simply shut down. If either is to be the case, then we want to gather as much information and proof as we can while the third portal is still active. I have been told by several well-placed researchers that the U.S. government knows exactly where all of the major portals are in this country. So, the report goes, the government is either purchasing the property surrounding some of the portals and closing the areas off or is intentionally destroying some of these portals. There has been some rather strong circumstantial evidence that does indeed corroborate this.

Several months before this book went to press, on May 22, 1995, the portal area that we concentrate our study on was sprayed with a substance that had a strong chemical smell. This took place late at night and was done from either a helicopter or a fixed-wing aircraft. Since 1993 this spraying activity around the country has not been uncommon. According to the Militia of Montana it has occurred and is occurring in almost every state.

In one incident in the western states, the sprayed material was retrieved by a doctor in Coeur d' Alene, Idaho. The substance had stuck to plant leaves in the area. When the mystery substance was tested in a laboratory it was found that the substance was of an unknown biological agent. It was felt that the substance may have been genetically altered. In the Sedona case, samples were taken from the area and at press time have not yet been analyzed. (July 10, 1995 update: A doctor in Prescott, Arizona, 30 miles from Sedona, has examined 16 people who have come to him and reported that their homes and ranches were sprayed from the air with a strong chemical-smelling substance.) Destroying the portal does not seem to have been the intent, as activity in the anomalous zone does not seem to have changed. In fact, activity seems to be accelerating.

To make my account of this portal activity complete, I decided I would have to include something about how it "feels" to be in close proximity to one of these energetic anomalies. The sensation of being in or near one of these portals is certainly unusual, and I say that because of what I would term an alien-feeling energy and activity that can be associated with these strange anomalies. It's a bit like being inside of something that feels and seems busy. In fact, that may be the case. It may be that these windows, holes, portals, or whatever they actually are, are in reality in the midst of a city, outpost, temple, ship, or some structure situated in the exact same place where one is standing on Earth, however, these objects may actually also be in another dimension or reality that is far beyond normal human perceptions. Human seeing and hearing apparatus can detect objects or sound only on very specific frequencies or wavelengths. It is now an established scientific fact that an object (or being) could exist in a solid form above or below our range of perception and we would not be able to see or hear it under normal conditions. We could theoretically walk right through one of these solid objects because its atomic or molecular mass would be arranged differently from ours, rendering it completely invisible and undetectable to our human senses although "it" could quite easily see us.

It is an eerie sensation, being in or near one of these portals when the portal is active. One can often feel energies moving about but it is nearly impossible to isolate or define these moving objects or beings. Could they, or it, be in a dimension that is parallel to our own Earth? Or, could it be that a twin planet of our Earth exists so close to us that we can occasionally detect its residents' activities as they go about their normal business? Or, could the portal be a temporal shift into a past or future Earth or alien reality? As the portal fluxes in and out with our own reality, does it produce solid projections in our realm?

Still further, could these strange portal creatures and objects be a creation of our own collective psyche? And if so, is it the Cosmic Plan for us to manage these creations, or life forms, in order to move humankind into higher levels of understanding? Or, could it be that these strange forms are in reality much higher than us and are in their natural state? Could they be ones that we think of as angels, ascended masters, or gods? Do these entities marvel at how blind we are, that they can cavort about right in our midst and we don't see them or make an effort to understand them? Still further yet, I suspect that in the long run the following may be the answer to what the

Sedona portals are. Science has now through the "String Theory" postulated that there are at least ten dimensions, or more, surrounding us that we are not physically aware of. A newer hypothesis is that occasionally there are semi-permanent passageways, or "wormholes," between the dimensions. Conventional scientists are at this moment very close to proving the actual existence of other dimensions and of wormholes. So if wormholes do indeed exist, now, do the residents of far-flung universes regularly visit us but we are generally unaware of their existence?

Wormholes and dimensions can also be combined with another scientific theory called hyperspace – or in simple terms, anything beyond our known cosmic reality. When Albert Einstein died there were piles of unfinished work on his desk, and what he was working on was his unified field theory. Had he proven the unified field theory (that everything everywhere is connected) it would have, and may yet, lead to the provable reality of hyperspace, multiple dimensions – and wormholes.

Strange things happen in these portal areas in a variety of ways. Last summer (1994), during a one-week period, I shot five rolls of film, a total of 120 photos. I used two cameras, and both were in excellent condition. Only about 30 of these photos developed. All were nighttime shots taken either with flash or five-minute open-shutter timed exposures. Some rolls were lost by developers, and in one case, frames were completely missing from a roll of negatives. Some of these shots I knew had something unusual on them. I had sent these particular rolls to three different out-of-town photo labs, so the finger can't be pointed toward one source. It's also odd that even under "normal" conditions about 80% of my nighttime flash shots developed completely black.

We all have had batteries in cameras or camcorders suddenly go dead while taking photos in these portal areas. Just days ago (May 1995) I had my Minolta 35mm SLR set up on a tripod to take time-exposure night shots. After several exposures the alkaline batteries suddenly went dead, even though my camera has a low-battery warning light. The warning light never came on. This has now happened twice. I carry a battery tester, and one of the two batteries was totally discharged. I often wonder if an alien life form is doing its level best to communicate with and exchange with us in these portal areas, and it, or they, are doing it in the only way they know how, resulting in paradoxes and mysteries creating confusion in our human zone of reality.

Chapter 2

Nineteen Points

The following is a synopsis of what I personally have been involved in and have been researching here for the past two years. The following (I call it my nineteen-points story) has had wide exposure already and will appear shortly as part of a story I wrote for a major international magazine. I am going to include it here because almost all of this activity took place in one or more of the three major portal areas I mentioned earlier. The nineteen points as written here have been updated to include all-new, current information and incidents as of July, 1995.

For credibility purposes, I must mention that much of this activity, as bizarre as it might sound, has been witnessed by some of the most respected and credible citizens of the local area. In fact, several witnesses hold positions of such high responsibility and authority that their credibility is almost beyond question. One out-of-town witness is in top management of one of the world's largest aerospace corporations. To avoid embarrassment to others, and as a personal policy, I never print real names unless specifically asked to do so. I often get information that no one else gets because it's well known that I will not reveal sources unless asked or allowed to by the sources themselves.

You will note that much of this information coincides with the information given by Linda Bradshaw in Part One but is presented from the perspective of my own research notes and personal experience. It does not invalidate her perspective in any way.

As Follows:

1. Frequent area sightings of moving balls of light, either silver, red, white, blue, or green. The sizes of these spheres have been approximately one to thirty feet in diameter. They have been seen to pulse at different intervals or glow steadily. The speeds of these objects varied roughly between 50 and 10,000 miles per hour.

2. Three reliable sightings of unknown animals, with no rational explanation of their origin. These animals were all four-legged, had either short or long fur, and their weight was between approximately 20 and 100 pounds. In mid-July of 1993 one such creature was seen by myself and a professional wilderness tour guide. We were in a jeep near Secret Canyon. This creature looked like a cross between a fox, a cat, and a raccoon. We got a very good look at it and we agreed that no animal like it existed on Earth. The animal was not a Coatimundi.

3. A number of strange tumors and inexplicable ailments found in rural domestic animals. And from two different horses in different places, a year apart, fetuses of four months each vanished overnight. Both horses were confirmed pregnant by a Phoenix veterinarian.

4. The appearance of highly unusual tracks. A number of six-inch-wide, twenty-inch-long, three- and five-toed barefoot tracks have been photographed. I found in an out-of-the-way area one perfect track of a soft-soled boot. The print was ten inches long and five inches wide with an inward-bevel sole. There was no tread on the boot. On May 20, 1995, a long-time local tour guide, while on an outing with a group of hikers, discovered ten unusual footprints near Loy Butte. The footprints were approximately nine inches long, narrow at the heel and very wide at the ball. Each track had *six* toes. The tracks were in dry, dusty soil and were in excellent, well-defined condition.

5. Many reliable sightings of single and multiple military vehicles late at night and in the dark, early morning hours. One of these was a convoy of about 20 all-white, numbered tractor-trailers. In one single, isolated incidence, uniformed (probably Army) personnel were seen and photographed. Every single report of these military vehicles has them going *into* the canyons. There has never been one report of them coming *out* of the canyons. Where do they end up and where do they go into without being seen? We haven't the slightest clue.

6. About half a dozen cases of strong oscillating vibrations seeming to originate from underground. In one instance the witness, a psychologist, said the origin seemed to be several hundred feet above ground. When active, these vibrations are strong enough to shake large structures and be totally distracting to the residents involved. These vibrations are seemingly not of natural origin.

7. A number of cases of human abduction by aliens. One subject was hypnotized by an eminently qualified psychiatrist. The subject, a local man, remembers being taken into a spacecraft, seeing almond-eyed, large-headed alien faces, and having something done to his knees and temples, possibly implants.

8. Strange nocturnal movements of unseen, seemingly humanoid creatures or beings. The typical scenario involves hearing footsteps, with no creature or intelligent being visible. Doorknobs late at night have been rattled and turned by unseen entities or agencies. Screams and howls have several times accompanied these visitations. At least a half-dozen witnesses, including myself, have had living, invisible entities about eight feet in height brush past them. It is a sensation of warm, slightly electrified water brushing past. These incidents do not fit in with the usual ghost or poltergeist activity.

9. Domestic animals terrified by things unseen. In one case something in a large open area of about a half-acre could be heard hissing loudly at barking dogs that were penned up. The hissing creature was

not a mountain lion. In one case a horse was found in its corral in a state of shock, and several thousand dollars were spent to bring the horse back to normal health. In a separate case, again in a remote rural area, a horse was found wedged into an angled tree. It was also in a corral and was apparently trying to flee something. Mountain lions, bears, and dogs can be ruled out in this incident and in most of the others.

10. A fire of extremely suspicious origin on top of Secret Mountain. Two thousand acres burned in August before the fire was finally doused. The fire was allowed to burn for five days before any attempt was made to put it out. UFOs and military helicopters and jet fighters were seen in the area at the time of the start of the fire. It seems to this researcher as if "someone" wanted "something" to burn and be destroyed – and perhaps it was. (More on this later.)

11. Late-night (midnight to 4 a.m.) overflights as low as 100 feet of airliner-sized aircraft and especially military helicopters. One particular daylight case constituted outright harassment by two military helicopters. The two helicopters left when a twelve-gauge shotgun was pointed at one of the pilots by a very angry local man. One of the helicopters was hovering ten feet above this man's house, which is located in a sparsely populated rural area. Along with this there have been unrelated sightings of jet fighters and military helicopters looking for something on the ground. This has typically involved about a dozen crafts. In two totally separate, unrelated local cases military helicopters had, in the distance, "something" completely surrounded on the ground. Witnesses were too far away to see what the object on the ground was.

12. Three completely separate, months-apart reports of jet fighters and one helicopter flying at low altitudes and simply vanishing. In one case, a mirrorlike flash was seen on the midsection of a delta-winged jet fighter. The aircraft had clusters of rockets under each wing. There was a flash and then the aircraft vanished and did not reappear. Type of aircraft unknown – could be some sort of hologram experiment. One of these incidents, a vanishing helicopter, was eyewitnessed by a retired Air Force colonel who remarked, before being angrily dragged away by his wife, "I'll be damned. They finally perfected it!" Your guess is as good as mine what "it" is. The colonel and his wife left the area before they could be interviewed.

13. One midsummer 1994, 9 a.m., incidence of a reptilian-like humanoid running along a dry, rocky wash as though trying to elude someone or something. U.S. military personnel were reportedly seen in the area at the same time. The witnesses were two adults and one seven-year-old child.

14. Voices heard in the desert at night, talking in a strange, high-pitched, chattering language. I was witness to one of these occurrences.

15. Jet fighters flying with (escorting?) a sphere of white light as large as the wingspans of the fighters. This comprises usually two fighters and one ball of light. There have been at least a half-dozen of these sightings in the past two years in the Sedona area.

16. UFOs trying to look like aircraft or aircraft trying to look like UFOs. I have, on many occasions, watched large and small aircraft change running lights into different patterns in a seeming effort to look like a UFO or something else. Why? I have also seen what I think was a huge UFO trying to look like a large jet aircraft. The craft, however, made no sound whatsoever. A number of people have seen that same occurrence in the Sedona area. I have also seen jet fighters flying in a defensive manner that, to me, strongly suggested they were expecting or were ready for an attack. An attack by whom or what in U.S. airspace? On the night of September 13, 1994, during a wild series of UFO sightings, I saw what looked to be a small, probably twin-engine plane coming toward me at a low altitude. With only the naked eye it simply looked like a small plane making an approach to the Sedona airport with its landing lights on. But when I picked up my binoculars and looked at it, it was a different sight altogether. In the middle, on the underside of the plane, was a red flashing strobe light. To the right and left of the strobe, and on what would be the middle of a light plane's wings, were two bright landing lights. But on the outer edge of each wing was a light that slowly pulsed with such a blazing brightness that at the peak of each pulse all I could see was the red strobe and a small inner portion of the "landing lights." It then turned east and flew right over Sedona. A

UFO trying to look like a plane or a plane trying to look like a UFO? Whatever it was, it was not normal.

17. One instance of three military helicopters chasing at high speed, at rooftop level, two fast-moving three-foot-diameter balls of blue light. There were multiple witnesses to this event that transpired right across the city of Sedona at 10 p.m. on August 25, 1994.

18. Three incidents where jet fighters were chasing UFOs. In each case the UFO was a sphere of white light approximately 20 feet in diameter. In two days-apart instances the UFOs turned and harassed the jet fighter by flying straight at it then making an abrupt 90-degree turn just before the UFO would have hit the fighter. Seems tempers might be getting a bit short.

19. Two more recent local incidents involving hikers or four-wheel drive buffs running into assault-weapon-toting soldier types and being turned back at gunpoint. This makes a total of about twelve of these incidents (that I know of) over a five-year period. These last two occurred on or about September 24, 1994. One was about a mile from the Sedona city limits and the other was in a remote part of the Coconino National Forest on the Colorado Plateau (Mogollon Rim), about 15 miles northwest of Sedona. In the typical scenario, hikers in a remote area run into two or more "soldiers" in charcoal-black uniforms bearing no insignias. The hikers, etc. are told in no uncertain terms that they are in a restricted area and are to turn around and leave the area the way they came. These soldier types in the black uniforms are almost always hostile, usually carry M-16 assault rifles, and give the clear impression that they will shoot if their suggestion is not carried out at once. They are not survivalist types or American Patriot Militia in training. Neither of these two groups has any idea of who the intruders in black are.

This 19-point saga continues weekly and monthly in the Sedona area and in many other locations around the country. One really has to ask the question — what *is* going on in our country?

Chapter 3

Believe Nothing

I t's interesting how "coincidences" occur. Seven years ago I went to a great deal of trouble to locate a copy (long out of print) of John Keel's book *The Eighth Tower*. A friend donated a copy of the book, and after so much effort to obtain it, I never read it. Nearly completing my section of *Merging Dimensions*, I suddenly had a driving urge to find the forgotten copy of *The Eighth Tower*. I went over to my cluttered storage unit and located the buried book in less than a minute. It practically jumped out at me. As it turns out, most of the material in *The Eighth Tower* addresses phenomena that are almost identical to what we have been experiencing and dealing with in the Loy Butte/Red Canyon portal area.

The universe works in mysterious ways. *The Eighth Tower* is an almost definitive comparison to our research team's mystifying experiences. I found, however, that I ultimately disagreed with some of Keel's journalistic and rather scientific conclusions. The reason for this is that since the 70s, when *The Eighth Tower* was published, a number of things have changed. Among them, in a positive way, is the consciousness of much of humanity. The following quote from *The Eighth Tower* is an almost perfect summation of my own suspicions of what this particular Sedona portal enigma may indicate.

> In the end, all paranormal manifestations may seem utterly meaningless. However, all of these weird events and games do have a subtle underlying purpose. They very efficiently provide a cover-up camouflaging the presence of the real phenomenon and its purpose. Penetrating that camouflage and correctly interpreting the true nature of the phenomenon could well be the final stage of man's evolution.

Governments and institutions will donate multiple millions for the study of the feasibility of a left-turn lane into a state park from a busy two-lane highway or for the study of the migrational and social habits of giant Patagonian jumping rock rabbits. But virtually none has been allocated or donated (so far) to certainly the most important topic ever to face the welfare and evolution of humankind: the in-depth study of UFOs, aliens, and all other related paranormal phenomena combined. It is all related. All paranormal phenomena are linked together by curious threads and they need to be studied as a package. As far as I know, no government agency or high-level organization has ever conducted a serious, ongoing, thorough investigation and research of these subjects in combination. And if, by chance or design, some high-level organization has, then they are not telling us, the people, what they have found out. The Soviets, however, did do a serious study of UFOs. After a ten-year investigation they arrived at the conclusion that UFOs are real — especially considering that three of their best MIG fighters were shot down by UFOs in three separate incidents during this ten-year period. Around 1988 the Soviet military ordered a hands-off policy toward all UFOs flying in Soviet airspace. A uniformed Soviet colonel has stated this on film.

Another area the Russians have pursued with vigor is that of remote viewing and telepathic communication over vast distances. Remote viewing is projecting one's consciousness or a portion of one's consciousness to a specific area or place to view what is there. The Russians' verifiable findings in both areas were phenomenal to the point that several U.S. military agencies instigated a crash-course (and probably incredibly expensive) catch-up with the Soviets and are now on a par with their capabilities. The Russians have been able to telepathically send messages many thousands of miles from one person to another with 100% accuracy. The Soviets took remote viewing and telepathy out of the realm of the occult and put it to practical use – military use of course, but it did open the door into areas that were once taboo. It has recently been proven that remote viewing by trained professionals has a stunning 86% accuracy rate. They are almost to the point of being able to read, from hundreds or thousands of miles away, documents locked securely in vaults and safes. I am able to do remote viewing with a high degree of accuracy. A major portion of my last book, *Unseen Beings, Unseen Worlds*, was devoted to this topic. I can't read documents in vaults, nor do I want to. These are just a few of the usually covered-up activities we are aware of. How much else have governments been up to that we have no awareness of?

The distrust of the American government by the American people is now at an all-time high and going higher every day. Government cover-ups of what they know about UFO and alien activity alone is certainly near the top of the list. Let's look at the 1947 UFO crash at Roswell, New Mexico, for example. Nearly 300 witnesses have now surfaced who were directly involved with the incident in one way or another. These witnesses are both military and civilian. None of these people say that what they saw was in any way related to a weather balloon. I've read extremely convincing written transcripts of testimony by individuals who saw, close up, dead alien bodies and ultra high, unknown technology wreckage associated with the crash. Weather balloon? Roswell is just one more cover-up incident that most researchers and a few of the public are well aware of.

Another cover-up is the government's involvement in the 10,000-

plus cattle mutilations that have taken place across the United States in the past thirty years. This was once thought to be exclusively the work of space aliens because of the super precise way organs were surgically removed from the animals (a small percentage, 10–20%, probably *is* the work of aliens.) It now appears from recent first-person testimony that some faction of the U.S. government has, in fact, been responsible for most of the cattle "mutes." Some struggling ranchers have been hit hard financially due to large losses of cattle to mutilators. Helicopters using almost noiseless new technology were used in these nighttime raids. I've talked to people who have watched these helicopters from a distance of a hundred yards – or less.

The cattle were usually picked up in remote locations and then dropped from the air after body parts were removed from them. The cattle were, no doubt, flown somewhere nearby and then dissected. One has to raise the question, why didn't "they" just go to slaughterhouses? They could have gotten tons of cattle organs, or raised their own cattle. The question again is, Why? What in hell is going on? Surprisingly a large segment of the U.S. population is still completely unaware or apathetic about cattle mutilations. One has only to look at close-up photos of a genuine cattle mutilation to become a 100% believer. In a number of mutes there is no blood either on the animal or on the ground. From expert testimony we have no technology that is capable of doing this. This factor has been well researched by mutilation investigators and this points directly to the likelihood of alien involvement.

Black projects. Our government has, to date, spent hundreds of billions of taxpayer dollars on super-secret military-oriented black projects. Virtually none of this activity has ever been revealed to or explained to the populace that pays for it. A partial list of black projects would include psychotronic warfare (mind- and weather-altering frequency devices) and numerous massive underground installations. One of these big underground installations in California has 400 cars that are used just for running around the installation underground. Big? Another black project is ongoing research on astronomically expensive military (and probably alien) aircraft such as what is being carried out at the "nonexistent" Area 51 base north of Las Vegas.

Part of this aircraft research involves particle-beam weapons development. Some of these beam-type weapons are already in use and are probably being used to shoot down alien spacecrafts. One of these active beam weapons is said to be in place at Eglin Air Force Base in Florida. I have a photo of this purported weapon and spoke to an Air Force technician who said he helped construct this device. Then there are the NSA (the National Security Agency) and FEMA (Federal Emergency Management Agency). Their main function is to spy on the American public by intercepting phone and fax conversations. There are thousands on the payrolls of the NSA and the FEMA. A government by the people and for the people? Has intense research into UFOs, aliens, and the supernatural or supernormal been a focus of some black project? It's likely.

The reason I mention this government activity is because it directly applies to many of us who do UFO research. Many of us have been watched and sometimes harassed. I have no fear of the unknown and what might dwell there. However, like a lot of people I do have severe reservations about the doings of our own government. I know what they are capable of. There is presently a great deal of printed material on this from a growing list of sources such as *The Spotlight, Youth Action News, The American Spectator,* and *The New American,* to name a few. At this point the best thing the U.S. government can do is leave private researchers alone and let us do our research without interference, especially by not creating elaborate hoaxes and leaking false information. My opinion is that private researchers are on an any-day-now breakthrough in alien/UFO research which will revolutionize the way we live on this planet.

In the past several years there has been an amazing change in the attitudes of the American people toward a number of things, especially a more open acceptance toward the extreme paranormal. It's a new open-mindedness of many individuals who were once steel-door closed to anything that was out of the day-to-day ordinary. And that may be attributed in part to innovative, rather radical TV programs such as "The X Files," "Encounters," "Sightings," "Unsolved Mysteries," "Star Trek," "Babylon 5" and "The Sliders." It was once said by an original thinker that science fiction may not be science fiction at all, but rather the human mind revealing absolutely real realms of reality existing in other times, places and dimensions.

A fairly new development for me, personally, is when people discover what I write about. There is usually a reaction of utter fascination and curiosity. This hasn't always been the case. To my constant amazement I am now even taken seriously by religious fundamentalists. A chance encounter with fundamentalists in earlier years would have resulted in instant friction. I am constantly delighted by, and amiable to, this sort of change. For a long time, if someone asked me what I did for a living I would be as evasive as possible. If specifically pressed I would simply say, "I am a writer." I would sometimes cringe because then, often, would come the "Oh, what do you write about?" Again I would usually be as vague as I could. I got a lot of funny looks from people. I developed this defensive attitude because of negative reactions by past individuals. I have had people go ballistically, blatheringly insane at the mere mention of UFOs or aliens or ghosts. These days I unhesitatingly state that I am a writer, a writer of the paranormal, UFOs, aliens, ghosts, that sort of thing – and like I said, there is almost always instant and utter fascination and interest in this subject, no matter who the questioner is.

The world is changing – fast.

In the rest of Part Two I will go into topics that may seem unrelated to the subject of this book. But I am endeavoring to assemble a strong case pointing to the reality of the existence of anomalies such as interdimensional portals and super-paranormal activity. And, involvement in the paranormal irresistibly involves a wide range of human foibles and belief systems. It's a tough sorting-out and realigning process, for anyone.

The deeper I get into research of the paranormal, the less I think like other people. It's not that I am better in any way – because I am absolutely not. It's just that primarily I see a danger in accepting anything of the paranormal at face value or not taking it seriously. The more I get into this fantastic enigma, the more I am sure some faction out there somewhere is trying hard, to see just how stupid and gullible we can be. And it's been going on for a long, long time. There is, I am absolutely certain, intentional deception and deliberate high-level disinformation on "someone's" part. It has to be some sort of a cosmic test – it has to be, particularly now. Seek the truth, and the truth will set you free. This may be the phrase of the times. The keyword is truth, and some higher being or group may be doing their level best to make us see and realize the genuine truth. The only way this realization will come about is for us to stop relying on external sources for life guidance and to truly pay attention to the personal inner automatic pilot. "Listen to your inner guidance" is a motto that has been around for a long time and may be the essence to provide success physically, mentally and spiritually in our present times.

Reading and listening to everything of pertinence is the only way we can build a database for the internal guidance system to decide what is relevant and what isn't. Because of ignorance or a lack of information, some of the world's most entrenched beliefs and institutions were created thousands of years ago by a few who had in mind only power and profit. It's been proven that many of these beliefs have no verifiable historic record outside of the original document or decree itself. Many of these dictums survive basically intact, even now.

People don't question. Here is a small example. Twenty-five years ago I had a three-day job (I got fired) with a company that sold thousands of acres of almost worthless land in a stark area of the Nevada desert for $7000 per 30-acre tract. After the company's high-powered salesman got through working the audiences that were brought in, hundreds of these 30-acre tracts were sold. The buyers were never told that they were not also buying the water, mineral and oil rights. Believe it or not, few even asked. The Indians and the government kept those rights forever. So the land was, in effect, worthless. The company made millions. There were no roads in most of the tracts, and some of the plots were on 40-degree hillsides. It was all completely legal because the oil, water and mineral conditions were buried in fine print in a confusing and complicated contract that most people didn't completely read.

To get the sales job I was required to go to several slick sales seminars given by slick salesmen in expensive suits. During one of these presentations the speaker said something I will never forget.

He said, "If you forget everything else I say here today, never forget this one thing: the world is full of sheep." I haven't forgotten that – and he was right. The world is full of sheep. The world is full of people who, without question, will follow the herd with little or no question, no matter which way the herd turns or wanders. Because everyone else is doing it, it must be the right way. Many of our social, governmental and religious patterns formed and solidified this way – somebody is said to have known better than we do, so we follow.

After a time, a few of us finally stop and say, Wait a minute, something's wrong here. It's then that the awakening and the changes begin. The individual stops plodding along routinely with the herd and breaks away and becomes one who is in his or her own power. Following someone else blindly or living someone else's life especially now is a dead end. The world is riddled with irrelevant information, and we have to be able to discern on all levels what is real and valuable and what is not. Discernment. It could also be termed keeping one's BS meter tuned up.

Here is another example of this sort of thing from my personal experience. I have for years been intensely studying information given in one way or another by aliens, spiritual beings and others. At one time I made almost a full-time job of this. After a while I noticed that the information given was often in black-and-white contradiction from one lofty, all-knowing source to the next. One entity or source will say one thing, and another source will say 180 degrees the opposite. Why is this? What alarms me most is that there are so many people who will accept like gospel what one source said and will initiate and follow that proffered information, quite often with disastrous results. But that accepted information was, and is, so often unquestioned by the eager recipient. I was one of these unquestioning follower types for years until in certain situations I sensed and openly felt that something wasn't always right. Now I question absolutely everything and assume nothing and I feel that I have gained enormously from it. Deep-lying, free-flowing, unbiased intuition is now, and always has been, the only way. It does not fail.

This is serious territory and calls for serious discussion with no sugar coating on it. I think we must take a much stronger look at beliefs and events than has been the recent fashion. I think the outlook for the future of humanity is awesomely good – that is, if we stop following others, become a unified community, and blaze a new route guided by goodness, love (compassion), intelligence, integrity, decisiveness and discernment.

An old Buddhist saying:
BELIEVE nothing because it is said to be of divine origin. BELIEVE nothing because a wise man said it. BELIEVE nothing because its belief is generally held. BELIEVE nothing because it is written in ancient books. BELIEVE nothing because someone else believes it. BUT believe only what you yourself know to be true.

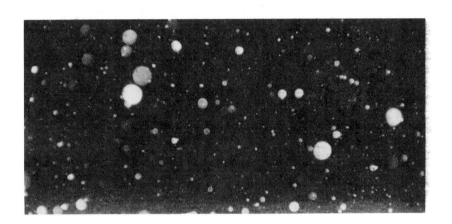

Chapter 4

Mysterious Lights

I want to cautiously include this following material because I think it has a measure of importance, particularly now. In the 1920s there was a theory introduced by Charles Fort, who is still one of the world's foremost paranormal researchers. I believe it would be of value to take a look at this extraordinarily unusual theory, even though it may well be without foundation. Fort's theory after a life-time of research was that we Earth humans are someone's property – a herd of someone's cattle.

It was an interesting idea, and one that has been tossed around by some of the world's greatest thinkers since Fort introduced this hypothesis in one of his books (all of Charles Fort's books are still in print). He postulated that we are thrown just enough tidbits to keep us satisfied and satiated and we are kept fighting amongst ourselves just enough so that we won't have too much time to think about a possible greater or different picture, a picture that may be better or worse than fits within our concepts of who and what we are.

This property idea goes against the grain of just about every spiritual, religious and metaphysical philosophy that is or has ever been. I've tossed this initially rather horrifying idea around a lot. But what if . . . just what if he's right? Let's consider for a moment that it may be an absolutely real situation, that we are someone's herd of cattle. If one studies religions and historical books, one will, in time, reach the conclusion that we have indeed been manipulated by an awesome power through wars, famine and prosperity since the appearance of Cro-Magnon man on Earth, out from nowhere, some 50,000 years ago.

What if some being or beings do own us and are herding us around, milking us of whatever they use or need until we get tired of it and revolt? Revolt, that is, in an awareness and intellectual sense. Then we are free. We will have earned independence under cosmic law. When we are free, then what lies out there for us? I think it would be more wonderful than anything in our wildest dreams: true freedom.

I think that whatever might own or manage us now wants to get rid of us because we are becoming an enormous liability – a pain in the ass. I think it is getting tired of us destroying and corrupting its investment – ourselves and its planet. Out of conscience and fair play it's giving us one final kick in the butt to wake us up and find whether we can see the light of awareness before it writes us off and allows us to completely destroy ourselves and what is left of the planet. Makes some sense, doesn't it? Even a herd of Holsteins, after eons, will get tired of being a herd of Holsteins and will, through decision and evolution, want to do and be something different and better.

I think the revolt has started. It has many current definitions, and I think it is going to reach a crescendo in the next few years. We shall see.

Perhaps I am wrong about some of the things I write about, but just maybe I am right, and if I am right, it may be of some lasting value to the world. When it comes to the wide open spaces of the unknown, I have no conditioning. I am a free thinker, so I am able to explore with no fear or false beliefs toward what I am dealing with or what might be out there. Free thinking is becoming a credo world-wide.

I believe the photographs in this book and the recent developments contained in it are the cutting edge of a momentum that now, most certainly, involves the future of humanity. There are many innovative, futuristic books on the market, but *Merging Dimensions* has a different slant from many of them. I think now is a time to make the most earnest of efforts to probe and understand as well as we can these opening challenges that are perhaps on the very borderline of human ability to understand or even comprehend them. These rather new developments are not present exclusively in Sedona, Arizona; they are happening in a number of other world locations as well. But the activity is focused or centralized in Sedona in a way that it is not in other parts of the world. Some examples of this world activity are the incredible Midway, New Mexico, daytime video footage of fast-flying creatures or objects, and the Sedona-like occurrences in the San Luis Valley in southern Colorado. There is the absolutely incredible 35mm and video films of close-up shots of UFOs in Jalisco State, Mexico, which, by the time this book is out, should have been aired on public television. Included in this are the recent widespread alien and UFO activity in Puerto Rico and the mathematically complex crop circles in England. Even more recent is the Pine Bush, New York, activity. The Pine Bush situation is quite similar to the activity in Sedona. A geologist has filmed detailed UFOs flying in the vicinity of Pine Bush, and at the time of this writing, startling new information and photos are coming on a regular basis from Pine Bush. So, in fact, paranormal activity is escalating dramatically in many planetary locations. In the past two years this new activity has been sudden and dramatic. Why? What's going on? Is someone trying to say something to us in the very strongest of terms? We can pay attention to it or not pay attention. With dismay I have seen all too often that this type of credible activity is regarded as entertainment, temporary like watching TV. In public apathy there is a danger or trap or failing that might become evident in the near future.

I am putting this in the strongest terms I know how because I think we are being given a last chance – an opportunity that may not occur again. My opinion is that time may be running out for all of us unless we take the bull by the horns soon. Are we going to look back and say, "If only we had . . . ."?

Following are some illustrations of recent paranormal activity in the portal areas of Sedona that I have personally been involved in. Most poignant by far, for me, have been the encounters involving airborne balls of light. One in particular is this first account. It has affected me more deeply and more profoundly than any other paranormal experience I have ever had. And there have, to this date, been many. My five books are full of these sorts of incidents and encounters.

Our research group has a CB radio network in the Sedona area in order to better track UFOs. This network is extremely effective. We can, within a short time, spread out and cover, if need be, an area of over 100 square miles. On one particular summer night we had spotted UFO activity, and I was in position near Dry Creek, waiting for several others to reach their outlying destinations in their cars. To the southwest, about two miles away and about 50 feet above the desert floor, I noticed a flashing white light that looked like a strobe light on an airplane. But this one was moving in a way that no light that was attached to an airplane or a helicopter would. It seemed to be a strobe light by itself and not attached to any other object. I began to watch the light closely with binoculars, and by its movements it seemed to radiate an individual intelligence. It would move about randomly, slowly and methodically. It would stop, go up and go down, and then it climbed straight up to a height of about a thousand feet above the flat desert floor. It hovered in that position for a few moments then it abruptly began to descend straight down. The light descended at a slow speed. I watched it as it went into a grove of ten-to twenty-foot-tall piñon pines and junipers about one and a half miles from where I stood. The light was now behind trees where I couldn't see it, but its flashing brilliance lit up a wide area of the desert floor. The light so brightly illuminated the surrounding trees, it looked as if the trees were covered with snow. Then the light went out.

I stood there outside my van pondering the whole thing when I suddenly noticed another object positioned directly above the strobing light on the ground. The second object was sitting completely stationary at an elevation of about 7000 feet (ground-level elevation is 4500 feet). It could have been a helicopter but it was too far away to make a positive identification. The second object had steady burning red and green lights on it and white strobe-like light in the midst of the red and green ones. I hadn't seen it earlier, but I had to assume that the second object had been up there as long as the white strobe light had been moving about near the ground. After the strobe-like light on the ground stopped flashing, the second helicopter-like object moved, or drifted, to the northwest and in about five minutes disappeared into the distance.

Ten minutes or so after the disappearance of the helicopter-like object, two, at first small, blood-red pulsing spheres of light came down from the northwest sky from about the same area where the helicopter object was last seen. These two crimson balls of light were so awesomely spectacular that it's impossible to find adequate words to describe the impression the lights made on me in those first moments. The red spheres pulsed independently with a slow five-second pulse then paused for a second or two, then another slow five-second pulse growing brighter and dimmer through the phase. The red spheres were descending at about a 40-degree angle. The spheres were moving at a speed of about 30 mph and at times were as close as 30 feet from each other and as far apart as 200 feet or so. This is only an estimate, as I could only guess at their exact distance and speed, but the objects themselves were about 20 feet in diameter. I say this because I was able to compare them with a ridge on Bear Mountain as they passed close by that ridge. Their distance from me at the closest point was approximately one and a half miles. I was looking at them with binoculars.

As in several sightings earlier in the year, these red spheres seemed to me to be living entities. They moved in a manner that was just too independently intelligent. They seemed like two entities, or creatures, accompanying each other. They in no way gave me the impression they were some sort of remote probe or some kind of mechanical or technological craft. As I write and think about it, they seemed to radiate a powerful animal-like intelligence. A rather basic observation, but it fits.

The balls of light continued their slow, gradual sliding descent, and as I watched, still utterly enthralled, they went behind a low hill several hundred yards to the right of where I had last seen the white strobe-like light. The red lights also went out, or turned off, and we did not see them again that evening. Our group gathered at my position on Dry Creek and we watched until about 11 p.m. that night. The lights did not reappear, at least not while we were there.

The UFO business doesn't pay much but it is never boring and it beats the hell out of watching TV!

I've written about these lights before but I think the importance of the presence of these lights just can't be emphasized enough. There have been thousands of encounters around the world with these phantom-like lights over the years. So many books these days are written on subjects such as spiritual self-help, how to ascend, shamanism, angels, and how to live a perfect life, etc. – all excellent, but to me, these lights and many other mostly ethereal anomalies are of the highest importance now. If we can comprehend and communicate with these creatures, or aliens, or whatever ultimate form they turn out to be, I think that what we could learn from them would stun us, or propel us, into a whole new and no doubt better and more productive reality. There must be a way to communicate with them directly and on a long-term basis.

The responses to my previous published writings on the paranormal have been about 90% positive. But on the flip side, I have been viciously attacked in print by a few book reviewers, letter writers, and others. These reactive comments have made me stop and think. After a bit of musing it seems to me that a few individuals' worlds of reality just can't adjust to the possibility of ultra-alien life forms living amongst and moving freely amongst us. My impression is that some critics think these life forms I write about are some sort of malevolent dark force or something else that is out to destroy us. My opinion is that that well-held notion is entirely not the case. I have been as close to some of these moving and stationary alien enigmas as anyone in the world, and I have never had but the most positive of experiences with them. Our own fears (and fantasies) are our only real enemy. Control fear, and wonder and fascination flood in behind to fill the void. It may be that these life forms want to communicate with us directly but our reactive primal fear of them keeps it from happening. And again, it also helps to be in one's own power, to be who you are and not living someone else's life or letting someone else rule your life to the extent you are not living your chosen and desired direction. Once a person begins to be, or really dares to be, who they are, they lock into a flow that opens up all sorts of unexpected and positive challenges and opportunities. It's a wild ride.

In February 1995, I had yet another after-dark light sighting that was not as dramatic as some of the others, but still impressive. We have discovered that things completely invisible to the naked eye will often show up stunningly well with night-vision equipment. These sightings, so far, have all been of skyborne objects. Ground-level lights, for some reason, show up poorly through night-vision equipment. The February sighting I had was as startling as it was impressive. At the time I had just obtained a new Russian-made night-vision scope and was experimenting with it. I was in a remote area of the local desert and I was focusing the scope on overhead stars. Using a precise series of lenses and electron tubes, these high-tech devices amplify night light coming to the eye through a scope (or binoculars) by a factor of about 30,000. In other words, the night-vision device turns night into day. Because of the electronics involved, everything seen through an NVD is in shades of soft green – a rather eerie touch in itself.

I was adjusting the scope, looking at two side-by-side stars, when I noticed that the "star" on the right was pulsing with a regular rhythm of one pulse every two seconds. A two-second pulse then a two-second pause. Many stars do pulse a bit naturally, due to distance distortion, but this one particular star was suspiciously odd and different. As I trained my full attention on the one pulsing star, it slowly began moving away to the east. Somehow, these pulsing spheres, entities, creatures, or whatever they are, know immediately when they have been detected. I would cautiously estimate that this pulsing object was at least 20 miles away from me, and by its actions, it obviously knew that I was watching it. These objects, when detected, very often move exactly like a wild animal hiding in the forest would when spotted by a human. There seems to be a measure of alarm and then slow retreat away from the area. Why? Why, at times, do they obviously not want a human to see them? Is it outright fear of us, or could it be they simply don't want to scare us?

I think it is the latter. In a recent late-night incident on Silbury Hill in England, five men and a woman had a sphere of pulsing red light slowly fly, as if curious, right up to them as they sat on top of the hill. The light came to within 50 feet of them, as if wanting to make contact with the humans. However, the incredible light retreated quickly away from the group when one of the six people became hysterical with fear. Fear drives these lights, or life forms, away. This same sort of encounter has also occurred in several other locations around the world recently. We, in our small research group, do not fear them, and want to make "face-to-face" contact with one or more of these strange nocturnal life forms.

I might mention, to be comprehensive, that several writer/researchers have inferred that these light anomalies are dangerous because of the arc welder-type of actinic rays they radiate. A number of people have been burned quite severely by these lights – I suspect through sudden, surprise, close contact. There may be a limit to how close a human can come to some of these lights. Depending on the size of the light, fifty feet would probably be a minimum safe distance. If the light is extremely bright, dark sunglasses would have to be worn to protect the eyes. The lights I have personally seen were not particularly bright: they glowed very softly.

These lights sometimes move through the light spectrum of prismatic colors as they first appear then disappear. I am certain that they know that their power, their brilliance, can be harmful to humans and that they can alter their frequency to be more accommodating. There have been many cases of quite close contact in which the human or humans were not harmed in any way. These lights can also become invisible. I've seen them do that. Maybe at the point of invisibility they are harmless to us. The only problem is that then we can't see them. At any rate, if some type of direct contact is made, it might be not with these balls-of-light life forms but with an alien life form that is quite compatible with our own. There may be hundreds of different types of these life forms out there. By the way things are going I think we are going to find out soon.

So the pulsing light I was observing with the night-vision scope started moving to the east. It seems the light was using the real star to the left as camouflage. The light was trying to look like a star. This is not unusual. See my photo of the "star" that moved three times sideways instead of downward. As the pulsing light moved to the east it changed speed and direction five or six times. The sky that night was almost completely clear, except for several small clouds scattered here and there. I saw that the pulsing light was headed for a cloud that was near it. I watched as the pulsing light moved behind the cloud. The cloud was perhaps ten times larger than the light. After 15 minutes or so, the cloud drifted several miles to the west and dissipated. The light was gone. It had used the cloud as cover, just as an animal would use a bush to hide behind and then run.

I now have one of the world's best collections of paranormal photographs. I was recently interviewed by a major national magazine, and of the amazing photos I have, the simple one of the star moving three times sideways, curiously made the deepest impact or impression on the hardened journalist conducting the interview.

There were times in the past when, having seen something like that light move and hide behind a cloud, I would have nervously questioned my sanity. But not anymore. I've had so many conversations with others who have had exactly the same types of experiences, and we know that what we see is absolutely real. Our subconscious minds are the problem, because the human brain has no way to relate to or conceptualize these completely out-of-normal adventures. For me, if the incidents or activity get to be more than I can handle or rationally deal with, I simply walk away from the whole thing for days, weeks, or more, until I can logically look at the situation and then pick up where I left off.

Albert Einstein once said, "The most beautiful thing we can experience is the mysterious." I can't agree more because once one gets over the primal human fear that these mysterious animated forms are going to kill, maim, eat or whatever, then an almost fanatical curiosity and fascination takes its place. One wants to know why they are, who they are, and what they are. I have now encountered dozens of these different physical and nonphysical entities. If they, any of them, had any intent to harm me, they or it could have easily done so long ago. If we honestly extend to them without fear, and stay centered and grounded, it seems they extend to us. I might add that a personal theme of goodness toward all things is an asset. Goodness as a concept has a beauty that transcends all ugliness in any form that it might take. Maybe it's called spiritual and personal integrity.

I'm still here and getting deeper and deeper than ever into these incredible mysteries and enigmas, and again I am convinced that these mysteries are of the greatest challenge and interest to the human race. We *must* know what these things are. Our future may depend on it. It's obvious, at this point, that the governments aren't going to do it (or cut us in on it), so it's up to us — the people.

Chapter 5

The Hotter the Fire,
the Purer the Gold

I am well aware that much of what I write about in Part Two might
seem utterly crazy to a few conventional minds. I've run into it in
the past so many times I've lost count. It's only when one comes face
to face, as I have, with one of these "life forms" that one becomes a
rather militant believer in these things — as I have.

A peculiar human downside of some of these sightings and encounters is the effect they have on the unstable or immature. I've seen a
lot of this now — too much, I suppose. It is not something I wish to
deal with anymore, and I avoid the situation whenever and wherever
I can. I am referring to those individuals who get involved in the
goings on of the paranormal but do not have their feet planted firm-
ly on the ground. It's hard enough to deal with the obvious realities
of these sightings and encounters without also having to deal with the

illusions and fantasies of adults who cannot look at a paranormal event logically and objectively. Maybe these people were a bit unbalanced to begin with and the appearance of a strange unknown pushed them over the edge and into fantasyland.

In a more minor sense are also those who can witness an awesome paranormal event and then totally deny that they saw it or who rationalize the event into something they can accept. I think these particular types have been programmed by preconceived notions, religion and parents – among a few.

I will now, if possible, interact only with mature and stable individuals when dealing with the supernatural realms of the unknown. It's my opinion, after years of observation, that many grown adults never had a real childhood. Now that they are twenty, thirty, forty or fifty years old and they witness something highly stimulating and highly strange, they have a grand opportunity to finally be a little child, with all the fairy-like illusions that go along with it. Believe me, this can get *very, very* weird. I just don't like to deal with it in the often exceedingly intense research I do. If I have the misfortune of hanging around one of these types long enough, I start to think like they do. And for me, as a researcher, that would in short time become fatal to my credibility. I feel fortunate to have had the opportunity to work with a great team of researchers. The Bradshaws and the others in our small team are perfect to work with. These are non-fearful, fun, well-grounded, curious and intelligent folks.

People often ask me how it is that they don't see the things I do or have the experiences I do. I always ask the question, "Do you look?" There is usually a long pause, and then comes the reply that once in a while, while going from their cars into their houses, they scan the sky for a few minutes or seconds. That doesn't work. One has to spend hours and nights in out-of-the-way places; then one sees and experiences. One has to go where it is happening – go after it.

Two days ago a friend came up to me in a supermarket parking lot with a rather amusing UFO story. It seems one morning he was reading the paper and having a cup of coffee at a local coffee house. He was listening to a nearby woman lament about how everybody but her sees UFOs. My friend offered the question, "Do you look?" Then he added, "Come on outside, I'll show you the areas where UFOs are often seen around here." They went out the front door of the coffee shop and he pointed to the general area of Red Canyon and Secret Mountain. Before he could say anything else, a large silver disk flew horizon to horizon, south to north, right over Sedona. The disk was moving at a tremendous speed. A friend and I saw virtually the same thing several weeks before that.

He said it was really funny – the look on the woman's face and her reaction to the sighting. He chuckled as he told me that she didn't stop blabbering excitedly about the sighting for an hour. For myself, I have to admit that in recent years the UFO activity around Sedona has become so commonplace that even I have lapsed periodically into apathy about these sightings. I don't even bother to write a lot of the reports down. They are soon forgotten. I caution others about apathy and I have fallen into it myself at times. The worst thing we can do is become blasé about an activity which is surely the most important single thing ever to happen to the human race.

The Sedona story has been unfolding a long time and will continue to unfold for years to come. Every week seems to bring a new, often different, and often startlingly dramatic episode.

During a ten-day period in January 1995 there were three amazing sightings here that I still puzzle over. This exact type of activity hasn't happened before or since in this area. All three sightings took place near one or more of the three major portal areas. The first report was from a woman and her daughter who had driven up to the overlook on Airport Mesa to watch the sunset. They remained, talking, after the sun had set. Shortly after dark they noticed a bright yellow object descending fast from high in the northern sky. The object was quite large, perhaps 50 feet long and 10 feet wide. As it descended and came closer, the object appeared to be bullet-shaped. The rounded front section was a bright crimson red and the cylindrical part was a brilliant yellow-gold color. As the object hurtled downward, it began to spiral in rapid, tumbling loops. It then leveled out over Red Canyon and Bear Mountain, still rapidly tumbling. It continued at great speed across the flat near Bradshaw Ranch. It was now at an altitude of about 2000 feet above the desert floor. The

UFO then gained about a thousand feet altitude, flew five more miles, still rising, and just cleared the top of 6000-foot Casner Mountain.

Shortly after that, from behind Casner Mountain, a green flash or explosion lit up the entire western sky above and around Casner Mountain. The green flash was immediately followed by a yellow flash. The flash or explosion was in the area of Sycamore Canyon. This is one of the remotest areas in the whole Sedona/Cottonwood region. If something was going to explode, it could not have chosen a better, more remote, or safer spot to do it. Jim Sweet and I saw a similar UFO-related explosion in the same place on June 8, 1995, at 11:30 p.m.

I've been asked, "Did you explore and research the explosion area in detail?" My reply was, and is, "I wish I/we had the time and money to do just that." There is not a lot of research or profit capital in this business, and there are even fewer individuals who are willing to sweat and expend time unless they think there is a sure profit or media payoff in it. Along this line is one of my pet peeves: film crews. This includes local network TV, national network TV, international cable TV and private documentary film crews. These guys roll into town and eagerly expect me, for reasons of ego or prestige, to happily spend hours, days, or in one instance, weeks with them so that they can get some spectacular and sensational film footage in order to sell their products, networks or programs. Financial compensation or publicity of my books is never brought up (except in one small instance). Now, I'm usually about as easy to find as a bobcat in a cypress swamp. It is a truth that there are people who want so badly to be seen on TV that they will do almost anything for it. Not me. Ego and prestige won't even buy me a cup of coffee. I stay in this business because of the fascination.

The second incident that took place during the first two weeks of January lasted only about five seconds. Most UFO-type sightings are of a duration of five seconds or less. The witness to the occurrence was a local woman was was not acquainted with the witnesses of the other two sightings. She said she looked up one night to see an orange ball of light coming from the southern horizon. As it approached the Sedona area it began a rapid spiraling motion. The orange sphere then disappeared behind Capital Butte, going in the direction of Secret Mountain. There was no subsequent explosion in this sighting.

Several nights after the orange-ball incident, a girl named Wendy, not acquainted with the other witnesses, watched a blue ball of light come from the east and fly over Sedona. This object did not spiral. It flew behind Capital Butte and "exploded" in the area of Red Canyon/Bear Mountain with a great, spreading blue flash. Curiously enough, this blue streak and explosion phenomenon has been, over the past ten years, one of the most commonly seen unknown flying anomalies in this area. Almost always the blue object explodes or flashes to the west of Capital Butte, backlighting it in an eerie blue light. These kinds of occurrences seem to happen in two- or three-day rashes, once or twice a year.

No doubt related to these incidents, I have in the past two years had two spectacular blue-green light experiences. Both of these sightings took place in the Secret Mountain portal area. The first sighting occurred in June of 1993. I was in the Dry Creek basin area. Just after 11 p.m. I looked up and saw a speck of blue-green light falling out of the sky directly above where I stood. As this light fell, it grew and grew in size. This entire episode lasted only four or five seconds. The blue-green light grew to a tremendous size and then it exploded silently in a huge fireworks-style ball of blue and green sparks. The silent explosion lit up the landscape for twenty miles in all directions with a phosphorescent bluish green glow. This first blue-green explosion was also witnessed by a local jeep tour driver who was camped four miles from me in Sterling Canyon.

My second blue-green ball sighting also took place near Secret Mountain. One night, about a year after the previous episode, I chanced to look up at the evening sky. A meteorite-like object streaked horizontally across the clear night sky and burned out or disappeared. In precise three-minute intervals, twelve more white "meteorites" streaked across the night sky in exactly the same path. After the twelfth "meteorite" had streaked across the sky, there was a pause of perhaps five minutes, and then in the exact same path the other white objects had taken, an incredible blue-green ball streaked across the sky and exploded in a fireworks type of display. A shower of blue-green fireballs fell toward the ground and burned out ten miles or so above the Earth's surface. It would take a lot of talk to convince me those were just meteorites. I think they were something else made to appear like meteorites.

This next incident occurred in September of 1994. I was in the Dry Creek area during a night of extreme UFO and jet fighter activity. Near midnight, as I looked to the west, two blazing spheres of chrome-white light skimmed across the top of Maroon Mountain, less than a half mile from Secret Mountain (the Secret Mountain portal was then still active). These two chrome-white lights flew straight in my direction in a magnificent curving arc. I did manage to get a good photo of these lights as they stopped and then hovered several hundred yards from my position. I snapped the photo a split-second before they blinked out. I caught them just as they were disappearing. What was most impressive by far in this experience was the dazzling, glistening chrome-white color the lights exhibited. This activity was also witnessed by Linda Bradshaw and her son Vic, who were at their ranch several miles to the south. I would be very interested in hearing from anyone else who has physically seen these chrome-white lights. As far as I know, this is the first sighting of its kind anywhere.

Also during that general time period, around the 15th of January 1995, I had one of the most unusual paranormal experiences I have ever had. It has nothing to do with portals, I am sure, but I will mention it as a strange experience of note. I cautiously mention it here because it is one of the very few paranormal incidents to give me a good fright. The only reason the incident scared me was because I was not prepared. I was caught off-guard and was still 80% asleep when it happened. (I camp out in the desert alone a lot and was camping that night in an area of low hills to the south of Sedona.) I awoke, for some reason, at 2:30 a.m. and immediately noticed a patch of bright light on top of a nearby hill that looked like a spotlight beamed to the ground. The sky was overcast that night, and there was no source of the spotlight beam that I could see.

For ten or fifteen seconds I studied the brightly illuminated area. It was perhaps 50 feet across and was near the top of the high hill. I glanced away for a few seconds and then looked back. The bright spot was gone. But . . . several hundred feet below where the bright spot had last been, a light equal in size was moving down the hillside. This other light was nothing more than a silvery shadow. I thought, "Is that coming toward me?" I stood there staring at the patch of dim light sliding along over the tops of the small pine trees and low brush, and it was indeed headed straight for me. I watched the patch of light long enough to be sure it was headed in my direction, said the hell with it, crawled back into bed and pulled the covers over my head. I didn't see or hear anything unusual after that, and after a while I went back to sleep.

I wondered, as I sometimes do, if I had somehow imagined the patch-of-light incident. Two days later I was talking to a local resident who had been out UFO-watching that night. I mentioned my strange experience. She said that that same evening they had watched a searchlight-like beam coming from the overcast sky. This was in the Loy Butte area, and this beam played about mountainsides and down to the desert floor as if it was looking for something. The beam was just a beam – it didn't have an obvious source. This is not something that happens frequently here. I know of only two other incidences of that beam-type of activity in Sedona.

In one case, in September 1994, a Village of Oak Creek woman watched a late-night UFO play a searchlight-like beam around the area between Verde Valley School and Bell Rock, the first portal area. A curious addition to this sighting was that the beam of light occasionally pulsed. Two years before that particular beam sighting, another Village of Oak Creek woman observed a UFO sitting directly above Verde Valley School (a private school). A searchlight-like beam emitted from the multicolored UFO, and the beam probed around the school grounds for about ten minutes. At that point the beam abruptly shut off and the UFO slowly lifted up and flew away to the south over House Mountain.

Two days after the September 1994 pulsing-beam incident, a young Village of Oak Creek woman was out sunbathing in her backyard at

1:15 p.m. She said she watched a jet fighter fly low over Bell Rock. This jet fighter was accompanied by two silver disks, one of which she said was not five feet from the fighter's right wing. The disks were about 20 feet in diameter. Then, several days after this sighting, two large military helicopters harassed a number of residents of that neighborhood, including her. The young woman told me that one of these powerful military helicopters came down to within several feet of the roof of her house. This helicopter-almost-landing-on-my-roof type of harassment is not at all uncommon after dramatic UFO sightings nationwide. Again, why? This has to be government procedure; what is it that they are up to?

On May 28 or 29 of 1994, a UFO/U.S. military incident took place near Sedona that drew an inundation of national and international attention. I have previously written much on this incident. To summarize for this book, I believe a UFO landed or was shot down by the U.S. military, or, a jet fighter was shot down by a UFO between Red Canyon and the city of Cottonwood. Cottonwood is 20 miles to the south of Sedona. For two weeks just before and just after May 29, the UFO, jet fighter and attack helicopter (Cobra, Apache and Huey) activity in this area was widespread and startlingly blatant. Even nonbelievers in the highly unusual were talking about these activities, and to this day, after a great deal of research, we can only conjecture about what actually, physically took place on the weekend of May 29, 1994. However, strong circumstantial evidence indicates the probability of a crash of an extremely, nationally, sensitive flying object. It very likely has something to do with one of the portals.

Perhaps I can't give a lot of answers, but I can certainly raise a lot of questions that need to be explored.

Chapter 6

Photographing the Paranormal

While my part of this book was in the early stages, the second portal zone in the area of Secret Mountain burned. Last fall (1994) there was a huge fire of extremely unusual and suspicious origin that burned across the tops of Secret Mountain and Lost Mountain. About 2000 acres were blackened. Jet fighters, military helicopters and UFOs were seen, prominently, in the area at the outbreak of the fire. The fire, which started on remote, unpopulated Secret Mountain, burned for five days before any attempt was made to control it or put it out. Smoke from a forest fire is usually black, white or gray, but several times, bright yellow plumes of smoke were seen billowing off Secret Mountain. Secret Mountain has long been the focal point of UFO and paranormal activity in the Sedona region. Since the big fire, there have been absolutely no reports, *not one*, of any kind of paranormal or UFO activity in the region encompassing Secret Mountain. Perhaps this will change in the future. It has been a common topic of conversation in the Sedona area that the fire seemed suspicious and perhaps was intentionally set. If it was a planned fire meant to burn something of a strategic nature, what was it that was burned? Could it have been an underground base, a portal, an installation, or a device that burned? Who knows. But the sudden cessation of high paranormal activity on that mountain after the fire points to some sort of an incident of enormous significance.

In late August 1994 I was giving a nighttime UFO talk to 18 women in a tour group from northern California. This was near Red Canyon. As I was giving the talk, a bright light from the southern sky flew straight at us at high speed then vanished or "blinked out." After some group discussion about the vanishing light, I continued with my lecture. As I talked I was watching two stars in the southeastern sky. To my amazement the "star" to the left suddenly made a complete loop, passing near the star on the right. The star then returned to its original position. I stopped my talk and said, "You know, I think I just saw a star make a complete loop." From half the women in the group came a chorus of excited exclamations. They had seen the same thing I had. They had been watching the same two "stars." Strange things happen around here.

If one should chance to run into some of the anomalies I have discussed in this book, there are ways to photograph them, if one wants to. There are several procedures we haven't tried yet, but I will run through all of the methods I know of and know to work under some or all situations. If one or all of these methods work for anyone who tries them, and a spectacular paranormal photograph is captured, I would like to obtain a copy for my collection. I would be happy to pay for the developing and shipping costs. I have now had a great deal of experience with a wide range of paranormal photographs, and in monetary terms there is really little value to the photos other than sharing them with others. I have had people show me photos they were sure they were going to get wealthy on. Needless to say, they still have them. I would have liked to get a copy, but neither I nor anyone else in this field will pay much for them. Authentic close-up photos of alien spaceships are now a dime a dozen. I probably have copies of most of them. Some of these photographs are truly awesome. The only photo at this stage that would be worth an undetermined amount of money would be a close-up, in-focus, photo or video footage of a live or dead alien or a live or dead bigfoot (preferably alive, of course). A photo like that, depending on what it is, could be worth up to $25,000, or *much more* if it's not a hoax - there have been plenty of those. I've been caught up in a couple of intentional hoaxes, and it won't happen again.

The first piece of equipment one needs for paranormal photos is a camera. I keep with me at all times a 35mm single-lens reflex camera and two or three inexpensive (under $20) grab-point-and-shoot cameras with built-in flash. The cheap point-and-shoot cameras are even better if they can be operated with one hand. I have a basic 50mm lens for the 35mm SLR and a 300mm telephoto lens that will focus down to fifteen feet. An ultraviolet filter, or a daylight filter, for the 35mm SLR is an option. I've heard that unseen daytime objects will often show up when an ultraviolet filter is used. However, I've tried it and I have had no luck so far with an ultraviolet filter.

If one wants to save money, photographic equipment can be bought very reasonably through almost any photographic magazine available on any magazine rack. A camcorder is the next piece of equipment. So much footage is now being shot with video cameras night and day that they are becoming a required item in a UFO or paranormal researcher's inventory. The smaller, the better. Any clunky equipment is out because fumbling with something bulky and complicated can easily cost a once-in-a-lifetime photo opportunity. The small and very expensive high-resolution camcorders are the best, but a much less costly camcorder will do just fine also.

Jose and Karen Escamilla of Midway, New Mexico (near Roswell) have shot much of their incredible flying object/creature footage by simply leaving a tripod-mounted camcorder running all day outside of their house. We have tried that here in the third portal area with good results. We *may* market a video on this activity.

The two procedures we use most in our research are nighttime

flash photos and three- to five-minute tripod-mounted time-lapse pho-
tography. Illinois resident Gary Hart, one of the world's top paranormal researchers, recently gave me an excellent tip I had not previously thought about. Most of the best paranormal photos occur
when nocturnal flashing lights are in evidence nearby. I'd best
explain these flashing lights before I go on. When you first see these
flashing lights, don't doubt that you are actually seeing them. They
occur in areas of high paranormal activity; they are actually quite
common. It took me a long time to convince myself that I was actually seeing these lights. They are very subtle, usually quite dim,
ghostlike and rather etheric in appearance. They are also quite
small – one half-inch and six inches are the smallest and largest I
have seen. The flying, pulsing lights are a different matter; they can
be huge.

These tiny flashing lights come in two colors – soft white and crimson red. I've only seen the red ones once, and the ones I saw were
indeed tiny. They were almost imperceptible and looked in a way like
the small, red flashing lights on a Christmas tree. We have been randomly taking pictures when the flashing lights are around and when
they are not around. Gary Hart's advice was to wait until the lights
start flashing then take a photo in their direction. We will try this.
I am also going to try Gary's advice with my 300mm lens with a three-
minute tripod-mounted time exposure. Evidently, some of the best
nocturnal paranormal photos have been taken with this 300mm-lens,
three-minute exposure technique using 400 ASA film.

We have done a lot of experimenting with all types of 35mm film.
Most of our photos are shot at night. We have had the best results
with 400 ASA to 1000 ASA film. Using 1600-speed or higher film all
the time can get costly. We have had poor results with film below 400
ASA. 100 and 200 ASA film is inexpensive, but avoid it for paranormal research; it apparently is simply not sensitive enough to
record paranormal nighttime anomalies.

The most extraordinary things happen when one gets deeply into
paranormal investigation and spends the night out in the dark. A
while ago I was out in the desert near the Loy Butte/Red Canyon portal (third portal). I was preparing to take some 35mm time-exposure

shots. I kept having unusual problems with the camera; nothing was working right. The night was crystal-clear and cold. Getting frustrated, I finally got the camera set up on the tripod and took two photos. Then the camera stopped working altogether. I fiddled with it for a while and got one more shot. Then the light meter on the camera wouldn't even work. I checked the new alkaline batteries with a tester, and both batteries were stone dead. This is a fairly common occurrence when doing UFO research and, as I mentioned earlier, it has happened before. I carry all sorts of extra batteries but didn't have one for the camera because the low-battery warning light will normally warn me days or weeks before I have to replace the batteries.

So I called it a night. Just then a silent cluster of six or eight brilliant white lights rose up into the northern sky. These lights were as bright as strobe lights but were not flashing. Spellbound, I watched these blazing lights and while I watched, two jet fighters shot up from nowhere and climbed to join the cluster of lights. One fighter was on one side of the lights, and the other fighter was on the other side. In less than a minute the lights and the jets disappeared into the distance.

The next night I was back in the same place with plenty of extra batteries for the camera. I had shot a roll of film and was starting on a second roll when I heard the unmistakable roar of jet fighters coming. I looked to the north and there were a half dozen or more fighters in the exact same place where I had first seen the blazing cluster of silent lights the night before. The fighters, probably F-16s, were doing something that I would consider highly unusual. Each fighter had on it only one strobe-like light, and it was steadily burning just like the silent lights of the night before. The fighters flew side-by-side in a perfectly straight line about 200 feet apart. I watched them fly about ten miles. All at once the white lights on the jets flicked off in perfect unison as if someone had flipped a switch. As the jets disappeared to the north, only one fighter on each end of the wide line of jets had a light on. It was a flashing red strobe light. This was just another one of those strange, unexplainable things that happen while doing paranormal research.

A number of pertinent updates were inserted into the finished manuscript of this book after the manuscript was nearly in its final form. The following is another. I've just learned that a man camped near Fay Canyon on May 9, 1995, witnessed a similar steady-burning strobe-light incident but his experience was far more dramatic than mine. My sighting was on May 5th. Fay Canyon is about two miles from my position near Loy Butte.

At about 9 p.m. on May 9, he looked up, and flying silently over his campsite were three bright red lights arranged in a triangular pattern. He said it looked like the lights were at each corner of a huge craft. He was not able to estimate the actual size of the craft. Minutes after the red lights went over, another sighting took place. He said that from the south came a craft with three rows of white lights on it. This one made no sounds either and was also flying at a slow speed. The lights were as bright as strobe lights but were not flashing. There were three parallel rows of white lights; each was about ten feet from the next light. There were twelve lights in each row. So the craft would have been 125 to 150 feet wide and about 60 feet long.

There were the three rows of white lights, and from the frontmost row, facing forward, were three lights that extended out about 30 degrees to each side of the craft. In these rows were two white lights, and at the outer end was one red light.

There are a few other photographic methods that are worth mentioning. These methods are quite exotic, and we have not tried them yet. One is radar-activated cameras. Unusual movement picked up by a small radar unit will start a camera rolling. This is expensive, to say the least. Another exotic method is heat-sensitive infrared film and infrared cameras. Infrared film is difficult to obtain and expensive and must be kept at cold-camera temperature. Also, fluctuating outdoor temperatures can drastically alter the effectiveness of infrared film. However, I have seen some absolutely remarkable daytime life-form photos taken with infrared film. I would at some time love to work with infrared.

One last photographic method we haven't employed yet, and perhaps will, is shooting photos through a night-vision device with a 35mm or video camera. This is entirely feasible and we are working on this idea with the equipment we already have. This sort of high-tech third-generation camera/scope military equipment can be bought ready-made, but it can cost upwards of $20,000 per unit for a good one. So we are going to try to stick a 35mm camera up to the back lens of our night-vision scope. One must be innovative at times. A good, basic Russian night-vision device can currently be had for about $500. A similar American model will be up to ten times that much.

Chapter 7

A Very Different World

Countless times I have said in conversations and in the writings I have done that I wish so dearly that all people everywhere could see or have seen the things I have seen and experienced. I'm referring to seen and unseen entities, and objects that are beyond our normal patterns of accepted reality. Many of these experiences I've had have taken place in the portal areas described in this book. My previous books are full of these various kinds of sightings and unusual experiences which I have had personally or which have often involved other people as well.

I wish I could somehow project it all on a giant screen for all to see and experience and evaluate on their own. This would be a very different world indeed if that could somehow be so. Why? First of all, it would jar people out of their present day-to-day sets of notions, beliefs and reality, and start them looking in a new, different, and probably more fulfilling and exciting direction. They would immediately abandon so much of the, in my opinion, useless things of life.

Mahatma Gandhi said that most of what we do in life is meaningless but we have to do it anyway. I'm not speaking of the necessary things of life – we always have to do those – but even some of those activities are relatively meaningless. Many things in this short life (this is not a dress rehearsal) are a total and complete waste of time. Repetition, over and over.

One only has to search one's life to find these nonproductive areas and activities. I will say that TV is one of these. Some others would be regional and national wars and personal conflicts and games, which can make life a senseless soap opera. If we don't learn from our past mistakes and those of others, how are we ever going to move forward as a species? What I'm driving at is that I wish more people would use unproductive time to study the paranormal, maybe then we would find some faster answers.

If people could see and experience somehow the things that I have, they would be so engrossed in the wonderment and grandeur of discovery and exploring beyond minimal boundaries of old patterns of living that there would be no time for conflicts or senseless games of any type. Perhaps sometime my fervent wish will be fulfilled, that all people will have, in a positive way, these inspiring paranormal experiences. Why me, I don't know, except maybe that it really is simply because I look. I know that there are plenty of people out there who would argue to the death about what I have just talked about. Not with me. Perhaps to them, what I say is meaningless.

I was in a metaphysical bookstore the other day browsing through a stack of books that had just arrived. I picked up a brand new book by one of this country's best known channels. Thumbing through the book, I came across a paragraph given by a channeled entity that says investigating the paranormal unknown and unseen is an utter waste of time. Naturally, that got my dander up.

I completely disagree with this philosophy for a number of reasons. Before I go into that though I must point out that I would always agree that chasing the paranormal to the neglect of one's basic life needs and requirements would indeed be a mistake. But few people rabidly charge after the unknown and neglect their life if they are normal people. However, that's not what the channel meant; the statement was that exploring the paranormal is a flat waste of time. In my hunt for certain answers hidden in the paranormal unknown, the experience has been for me anything but pointless. It has been a priceless learning experience. Dealing with and controlling fear is right at the top of the list of benefits. Fear in many ways is a complete illusion. Uncontrollable fear is certainly a detriment in any situation where it presents itself. And, in dealing with The Unknown, if a serious researcher doesn't learn to be logical, sensible, centered and well-grounded, he or she won't last long in the business. The paranormal weeds out the loose stones real fast.

Due to what I have had to deal with in the past ten years, in a human sense, I probably have acquired a symbolic Ph.D. in psychology. I have had numerous profoundly frank discussions with psychiatrists and psychologists about the reality of the paranormal unknown and the effects of the paranormal on human behavior. In this business, self-psychoanalysis is ultimately unavoidable. One thing I have discovered is that all psychologists are as fascinated about the unknown as I am. I haven't run across one yet that wasn't. I can't say the same about psychiatrists. This may be because psychiatrists are clinically oriented doctors and their minds are too rigid in certain areas. I will always maintain that life can be the greatest adventure, whereby one can combine one's life lessons with the exploration of the paranormal unknown. It's an ultimate challenge.

Are we, as a race, on the verge of a sudden and radical quantum leap of change? From what I have seen and personally experienced, I think that that is now a distinct probability. I think that those who are not prepared in an awareness sense for this change are going to have a difficult time making the adjustment if and when the big change occurs. It doesn't matter whether one wants to call it the Second Coming, the New Age, the fourth dimension, or whatever. By any definition, it's going to be a big change. We shall see – and probably soon.

Some Final Thoughts

I want to know what's going on. Period. I will go after it aggressively, with little or no fear and with an unwavering determination. Over the past ten years I have watched many others in this business, and over and over I have noticed that the few that get into trouble are usually those who have little or no spiritual beliefs. It has become obvious that if a person has strong, positive and gentle spiritual beliefs, there is a great power and protection in that attitude or stance. I have seen the power of spirituality work time and time again.

I hesitate to bring this next subject up but I have seen a lot of it. Somewhat in indirect concert with the last paragraph, I think by now we have all heard the expression, "All heart and no head." I believe it's a bit of a trap not to be balanced in both heart and mind. All head, or mind, is just as bad. This balance of heart and mind relates to the study of the paranormal just as it does in any other everyday human endeavor. A balance of heart and mind seems to be necessary to tune into frequencies of the unknown. Then it works productively.

Regarding the primary subject of this book, portals, I think that contact and interaction with the inhabitants of these and other probably limitless realms of existence is completely possible and safe now. The clear possibility, even need, exists because of the rapid, upward expansion of the consciousness of much of humanity. This is a condition that did not exist even ten years ago. But, again, until we can control fear, I don't think they will come to us on a mass or personal level. I have been close enough to these life forms to know without any doubt that they have vast, encompassing amounts of cosmic wisdom and information that we, particularly at this tenuous time, desperately need. An essence of "them" has, by association and proximity, rubbed off on me and stays with me at all times. I have gained a primitive understanding of who they are.

Most of "them" (they may be nearly limitless in divergent numbers) do not speak English or any human language. Our human languages are slow, tedious and inaccurate word systems. They of the unseen have, universally, a language system of their own. It is a silent psychic language. It is a telepathic thought and image transmission process. Some of these beings will, or can, transmit in words, but not many; most use the thought and image transmission process. This is something we as a species will have to learn and develop.

Whoever in the world initiates open and ongoing direct contact with the Cosmics first is going to have to become familiar with, and comfortable with, the awesome power that most of them inherently possess. It's not power in a negative, destructive sense, but sheer power in a cosmic, universal sense. Limitless power. That's how most of them exist — by directing and utilizing limitless cosmic power to travel and create with. They understand the responsibility of limitless power; we don't, not yet. Being centered comes into vital prominence here. Because their power is so great it can tend to be destabilizing in a human sense — particularly if one is just inches away from one of these beings.

Imagine what these magnificent dwellers of the unseen (no matter who they are) might be able to tell us if they wish. I think they are ready. I hope they think we are ready. We do, indeed, now have the abilities and opportunity to deal with these cosmic neighbors. To do so we will have to make many conceptual adjustments and jettison a raft of past beliefs that we hold in order to be part of this conjoining process and activity.

Why, I have been asked often, have they avoided direct and open contact with us before? Probably because we simply have not been ready. I think they are ready now.

Are we?

Merging Dimensions

Afterword

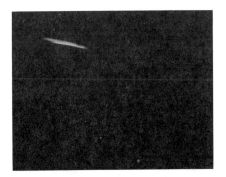

June 10, 1995. As I mentioned in Part Two, a number of pertinent items, sightings and incidents were added to the manuscript of this book after it was completed and ready to go to the printers. That's the UFO/paranormal biz. Things happen on a random, clustered basis, and when writing a book like this, one has to be adaptive and creative at rearranging manuscripts as one goes along.

The Pine Bush, New York, geologist (Dr. Bruce Cornet) I talked about earlier has a video and some still photos, which I have just seen, that prove conclusively, to me, that alien spacecraft do indeed disguise themselves as common propeller- and jet-driven Earth aircraft. I have long suspected this, and now I am absolutely certain that many of the unusual jet and propeller aircraft I have seen were actually, indeed, alien crafts. They even make proper jet aircraft sounds and propeller sounds to complete the camouflage. This I have long suspected also.

I experienced a sighting last summer, with photos, that was awe-some to say the least. I now know that what I was looking at was not of this Earth. Bruce Cornet and Linda Crystal have a close-up video of the same craft flying over them at almost point-blank range near Pine Bush. Linda Crystal took the video footage. It's identical to the craft I saw near Sedona. The ship I saw was about 100 yards across and 50 yards long. It had a cluster of about 20 white lights in its cen-ter and it was basically a delta or boomerang shape. I'm not sure whether Dr. Cornet's convincingly scientific video is available com-mercially at this time, but I'm sure it will be turning up in various UFO video catalogs in the near future. There is so much credible UFO and paranormal evidence out there now on dozens of videos, I often wonder what it is going to take to finally convince people that "they are here."

Almost daily, Linda Bradshaw and I are discovering new things about photographing the paranormal. One of the things we discov-ered several weeks ago (and this is startling and brand new) is that things of the unseen will often reflect light from a camera flash bulb. They will literally flash back – it may be intentional or unintentional on their part. It's true that we have discovered a concentration of these phantom-like anomalies, mostly in the third portal area, but I am absolutely sure it would not be too difficult to find many of these anomalous areas anywhere in the world. Linda and I have repeated-ly seen tiny, or large, flashes of light in the airspace above us or around us as we took flash photos. At first one dismisses it lightly, thinking it's something in one's eyeball or, in my case, the particles in my glasses. As it turns out, that is entirely not the case. I will go into this more, and I wish I could explain it in precise, analytical sci-entific detail as some researchers have already asked, but I can't – I've at this time no clear idea what this is or where it will lead. We want to pass these brand-new discoveries on now so that others can try them if they wish.

Linda and I do what might be called team photo flashing. We stand near one another and take random flash photos in any direc-tion; straight up, straight down, forward, backward, between the knees, hip-level – any direction. We might be walking forward and take a flash photo backward, or jerk the camera up and shoot a random photo in any direction.

These return flashes often look like tiny diamonds in the air. There can be as few as one or as many as a dozen or more. And once in a while we get a return flash from open airspace, which looks like we are taking flash photos in front of a mirror. Again, you can rationalize it as something reflecting in your eyeball, but after we each had witnessed these occurrences many times, we knew we were on to something. I need to add at this point that when a return flash is seen, that's usually not what appears on film. It can be a large globe of light, a tiny light, a red streak, a spiraling light, an object – or just about anything.

In a number of instances we got a flash-back which really is like taking a flash photo in front of a mirror but not exactly. These larger mirror-like flash-backs are usually three to fifteen feet away, six inches in diameter, and appear as if the mirror you are taking a picture into is broken into hundreds of small shards that don't reflect light straight back but instead diffuse it in many forward directions. Also, the return flash may not be directly in front of the camera but may be 40%, or 60%, or more off to either side and out of the photo range of the camera, though you see the flash with your eyes.

It's increasingly obvious also that these lights, flashbacks and objects we have been dealing with are of the highest order of intelligence. They are playing cat-and-mouse with us. They are giving us a puzzle piece by piece. When they want to be photographed, something shows up on film. And, they seem to know what we are thinking and to be able to anticipate every move we make. I surmise that they are able to manipulate time in some way. What is the next step? What will happen next? I wish I knew.

On a number of occasions we have mentally/meditatively tried to "call them in." This either works or it doesn't. "They" always seem to know when we are going to be there and where we are, and then they show up if they want to. It has taken many months of experimenting and thousands of photographs to discover this.

Linda and I have tried to catch them off guard and I got a definite feeling that this aggressive, rather impolite attitude on our parts irritated them somewhat. One night we developed a technique of putting a thumb or finger over the red or green light on the camera that shows when the flash unit is powered up. We still do this regularly. The camera's flash-ready light is very bright in the dark, and an unseen entity could quite easily stay out of the way by simply watching the red or green light on the back of the camera. We have also learned that these entities can move suddenly and at fantastic speeds. So we got really clever one night and covered the red or green light with a piece of black tape and then, in an instant, jerked the camera up or around and shot flash photos in random directions. This technique has occasionally worked, but we got the sense that they don't like it so we have gone back to being more casual and far less aggressive so that they can "pose" if they wish.

They indeed seem to know at all times what we are thinking, so any surprise tactic is probably fruitless or a waste of time anyway. If you try these tips, good luck with them, and let us know if you get any shots like we have been getting. So much mail is generated by a book that we cannot answer general inquiries, particularly long ones. But we will respond if the photo or matter is important enough.

The Men in Black are Back

On June 5, 1995, we had yet another soldier-type/hiker confrontation. This time it was in Fay Canyon. All of Sedona's ten canyons are arranged somewhat like the spokes on half of a wagon wheel, and Secret Mountain is the hub. All are in quite close proximity to each other. Fay Canyon is in the middle. At midday on June 5, a man from Albuquerque, New Mexico, had hiked back and was quietly meditating two-thirds of the way into Fay Canyon. He had climbed up to a rock ledge and had been meditating for some time when without warning he was confronted by two soldier types dressed "entirely in black." They told him he had to leave immediately and was to go back the way he had come. He refused, saying he was in a national forest and he wasn't going anywhere. This went on for a while, and the argument escalated. In a sudden move the soldier-types grabbed the New Mexico man and "escorted" him all the way back to his car, which was over a mile away. By the tone of the soldier-types' conversation, it was all too obvious there was something they did not want the man to see. In every confrontation case of this sort it's clear that there is something the military types do not want people to see. This, whatever it may be, must be temporary and intermittent and have the capability to develop or appear in any of the canyons. Curiously, three of these incidents in the past were not in the canyons but were up on the Colorado Plateau or out in the desert near Sedona.

On June 9, 1995, an even more recent men-in-black incident occurred. This time two off-duty policemen were involved. I am currently chasing this story down. They were hiking in Loy Pass ten miles west of Sedona and ran into two soldier-types dressed in black. The two policemen had the same reaction as the New Mexico man.

Allegedly, the hikers said, "We are police, we aren't going anywhere." The reply from the men in black was – rifles levelled – "*We have jurisdiction here!*" The police at that point didn't argue, and left the area.

One in a thousand hikers who ventures into the canyons has an experience like this, but when whatever it is, is active, it is dangerous. I spend a great deal of time in the canyons and have never run into these M-16-toting camo or all-in-black military types. I have no provable, specific idea what it is that they are prepared to get physical over and remove people forcefully from an area to protect it. A good bet would be that it is an opening and/or closing portal, or a tunnel. There have now been fifteen of these incidents in the past seven years. My guess is, the actual number of incidents has been in the neighborhood of forty or more. Most of the incidents I have heard of involved the experiencer(s) hurriedly leaving the area and mentioning the encounter in passing to a store clerk or a gas station attendant.

I have recently learned a little more about who these dressed-in-black goons are: they are a faction of the U.S. military. They carry U.S. military ID and are under the jurisdiction of FEMA – the Federal Emergency Management Agency. The beat goes on . . .

The Men in Black are Back

PHOTO: LINDA BRADSHAW

The Photo Section

In these photos is a yellow/orange bar of light on top of Jim Sweet's head, who was, at the time, shooting camcorder footage. In the other three photos the blazing light is hovering very near Jim. He remarked that at times he did feel the closeness of a presence, although this object was not visible to the naked eye. The balls of light between Tom Dongo and the pickup truck were also invisible to the eye but not to the camera.

PHOTO: LINDA BRADSHAW

PHOTO: LINDA BRADSHAW

PHOTO: LINDA BRADSHAW

PHOTO: LINDA BRADSHAW

PHOTO: LINDA BRADSHAW

This is our extreme mystery photo. Here is a 400% enlargement of a flash photo taken during the second week of June, 1995. In the shadows at the bottom of the photo is "someone" who does not resemble any of us who were in the area at the time the photo was taken.

The figure in this photo has a pushed-forward head, an extremely long, angular face, low tipped-back "Spock-like" ears – and – glowing orange eyes. We all talked it over. It wasn't one of us.

The "Flame" photo.

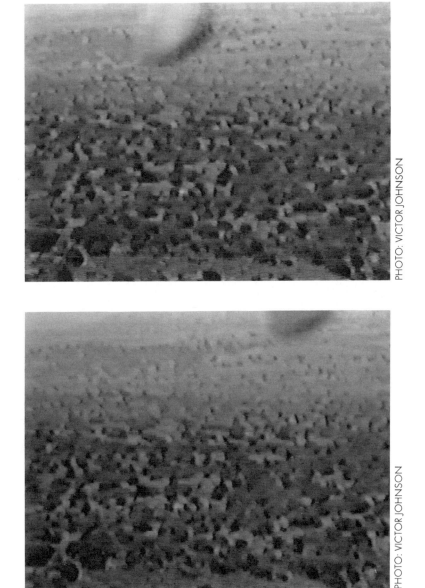

PHOTO: VICTOR JOHNSON

PHOTO: VICTOR JOHNSON

This daytime video footage (above and bottom left) was shot by Victor Johnson and shows an unseen object moving past the camera at a speed of several thousand miles per hour.

PHOTO: TOM DONGO

This photo was taken at night (full moon) with a five-minute open shutter. The objects in the center are stars moving in a normal trajectory. However, there is a "star" in the upper left that is moving horizontally and shows at least three stop-and-start motions.

This photograph has become more interesting since the time it was taken because of several ensuing developments. In the left center of the photo is what appears to be the face of a very large bird. Two almond-shaped, bird-like eyes are clearly visible along with the top part of a long beak and a tuft of feathers over and behind the eyes.

Just before this photo was taken a five-foot-tall bird was seen at night on the ground near the portal by Vic Johnson.

A week after the photo was taken, a woman from Phoenix called Linda and reported that she had seen a five-foot-tall bird. This bird in both cases closely resembled a garden-variety sparrow or finch — just extremely large. In the second case the sighting was in clear daylight in a thickly populated area of Phoenix. The woman is devoutly religious and before the sighting did not believe in paranormal occurrences.

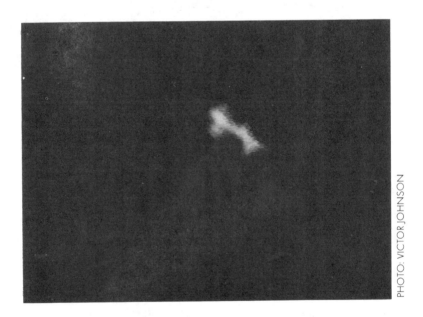

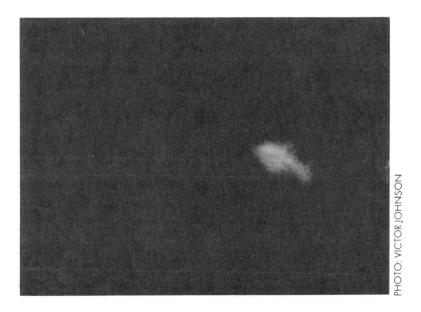

PHOTO: VICTOR JOHNSON

These pictures (above and left) are video footage also taken by
Victor Johnson. They show an illuminated flying object
moving past the camera at a speed of about
4,000 miles per hour.

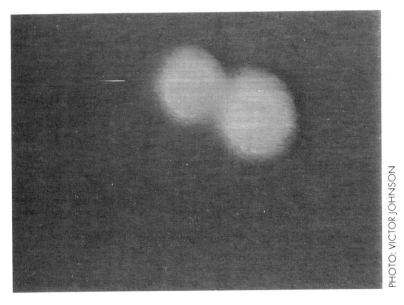

PHOTO: VICTOR JOHNSON

Balls of light (above) are a flame-red color.

PHOTO: LINDA BRADSHAW

feet

ad

Above and below: Body print left by Big Girl

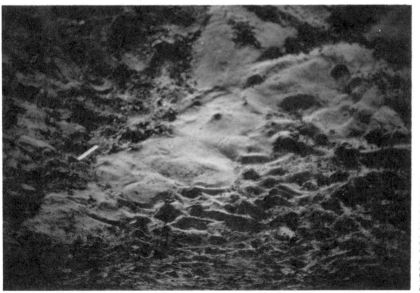

Merging Dimensions

PHOTO: TOM DONGO

PHOTO: LINDA BRADSHAW

150

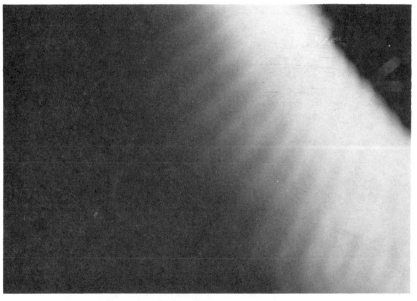

PHOTO: TOM DONGO

Jim Sweet
photographing
moving lights.

PHOTO: TOM DONGO

PHOTO: LINDA BRADSHAW

PHOTO: LINDA BRADSHAW

PHOTO: LINDA BRADSHAW

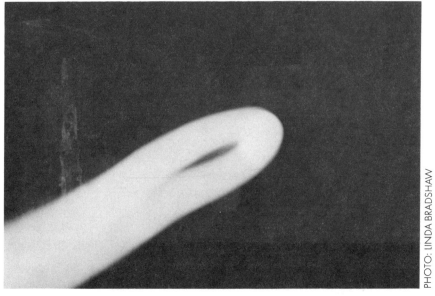

PHOTO: LINDA BRADSHAW

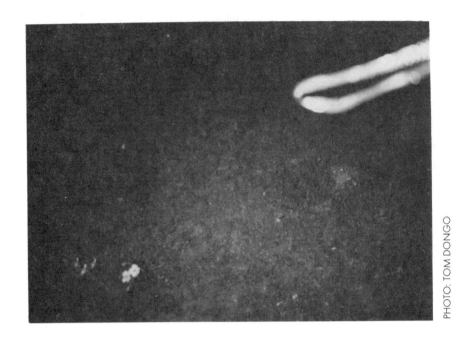

PHOTO: TOM DONGO

PHOTO: LINDA BRADSHAW

Photo Section

PHOTO: LINDA BRADSHAW

PHOTO: LINDA BRADSHAW

PHOTO: TOM DONGO

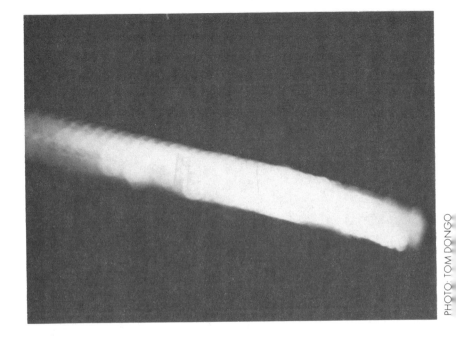

PHOTO: TOM DONGO

PHOTO: LINDA BRADSHAW

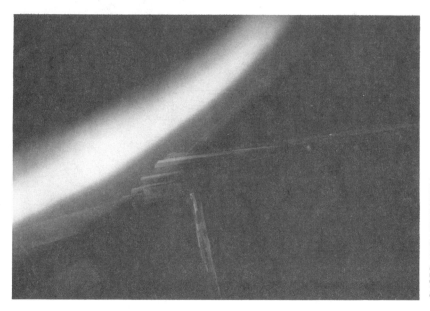

PHOTO: LINDA BRADSHAW

Mystery
shadow
in center.

PHOTO: LINDA BRADSHAW

PHOTO: LINDA BRADSHAW

PHOTO: LINDA BRADSHAW

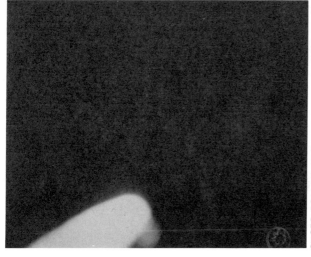

PHOTO: TOM DONGO

159

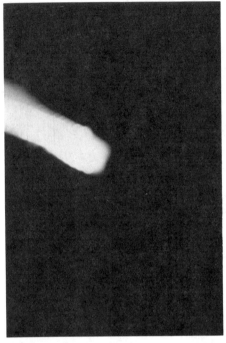

PHOTO: TOM DONGO

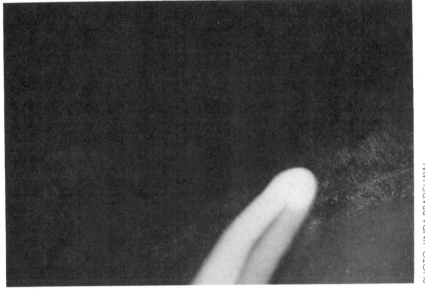

PHOTO: LINDA BRADSHAW

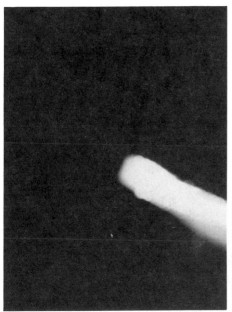

PHOTO: LINDA BRADSHAW

PHOTO: TOM DONGO

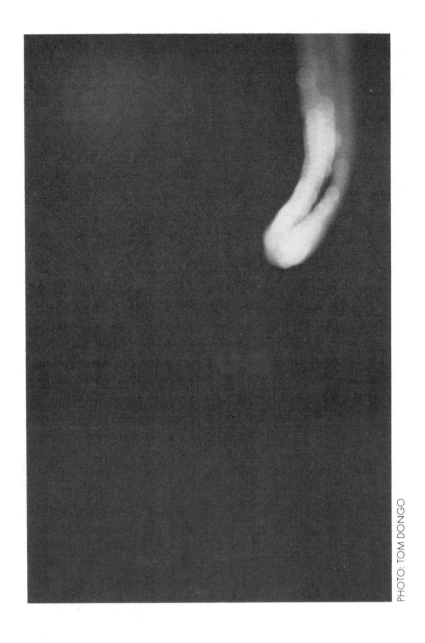

PHOTO: LINDA BRADSHAW

A presence was felt when this photo was taken.

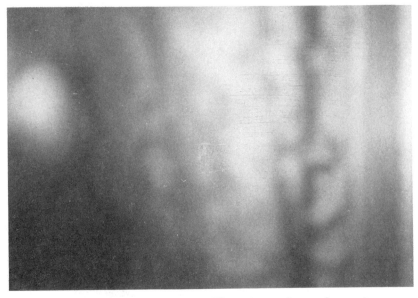

PHOTO: VICTOR JOHNSON

Energy photographed when Victor's truck was bouncing.

Energy photographed when Victor's truck was bouncing.

Energy photographed when Victor's truck was bouncing.

PHOTO: LINDA BRADSHAW

Mist that Linda walked through with window to the left.

PHOTO: TOM DONGO

<mark>off</mark>

Merging Dimensions

PHOTO: TOM DONGO

PHOTO: LINDA BRADSHAW

166

PHOTO: LINDA BRADSHAW

PHOTO: LINDA BRADSHAW

PHOTO: LINDA BRADSHAW

PHOTO: LINDA BRADSHAW

Tom Dongo meditating on white light as an experiment.
A white ball of light appeared on the photo.

Photo Section

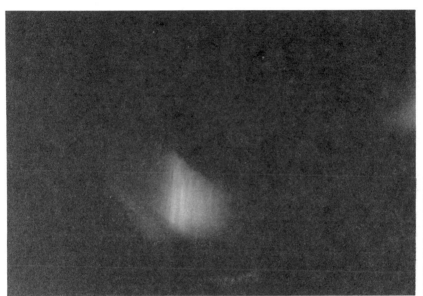

PHOTO: LINDA BRADSHAW

PHOTO: LINDA BRADSHAW

169

PHOTO: LINDA BRADSHAW

PHOTO: LINDA BRADSHAW

PHOTO: LINDA BRADSHAW

PHOTO: LINDA BRADSHAW

PHOTO: LINDA BRADSHAW

PHOTO: LINDA BRADSHAW

Photo Section

PHOTO: LINDA BRADSHAW

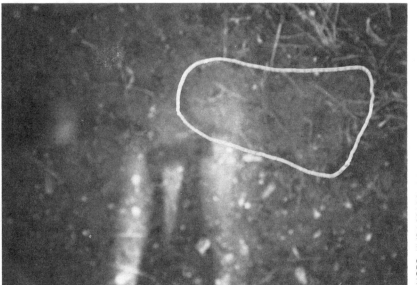

PHOTO: LINDA BRADSHAW

Huge barefoot track (outlined in white ink).

Bigfoot print in soft sand.

Bigfoot print.

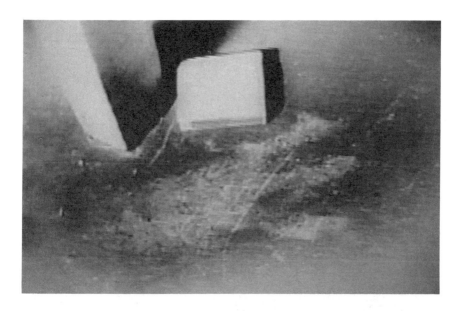

This is a photo of a large, three-toed, barefoot print discovered in
floor dust at a nuclear material disposal site in Russia.
Note the similarity to the track in Linda Bradshaw's photo
on page 176.

PHOTO: LINDA BRADSHAW

The Guy

On the following pages is evidence of a phenomenon that is yet another enigma we have encountered. We call it "the guy." It seems we have photographed parts of a male entity who is invisible to the eye but who shows up quite well on film. We have now shot over a thousand photographic frames trying to get the whole person but we have not succeeded. So we have legs, shoulders, the top of his head and bits and pieces of apparel.

We have rigorously eliminated any possibility of these photos being any part of Linda, myself or anyone else on our photo team. You will note on the forehead photo the being was less than two feet in front of my camera when the photo was shot. As I, Tom Dongo, am 6'3" tall, he would be approximately 5' or 5'2" in height.

At the time this photo was taken, there was nothing in front of me but an open, level, grassy field. An added curiosity factor is that the head seems to be wider than normal for a human – if that is what he is, or was. Even more curiously there is a bony bump or ridge on either side of the forehead. On the right side is a finger. I think he realized I had a camera in my hand and was bringing up his left hand to cover his face from the flash. Or . . . in a humorous vein, he might have been giving me the finger. Maybe they have a better sense of humor than we think.

You will also notice that on the photo of the pants legs there is the strange flying object hovering in the background that we call "the little UFO." Is the man an alien and not a ghost? I think he is indeed an alien.

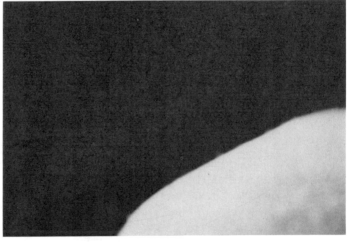

PHOTO: LINDA BRADSHAW

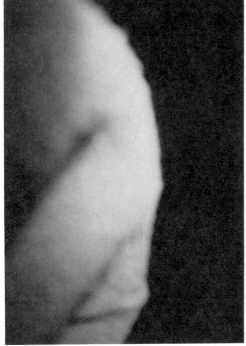

PHOTO: TOM DONGO

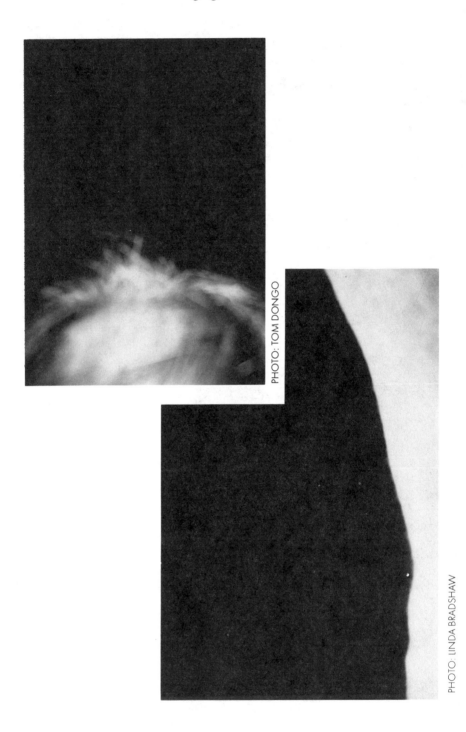

PHOTO: TOM DONGO

PHOTO: LINDA BRADSHAW

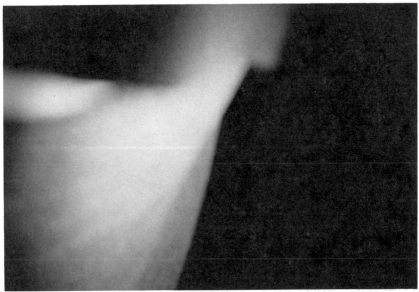

PHOTO: LINDA BRADSHAW

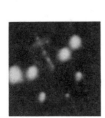

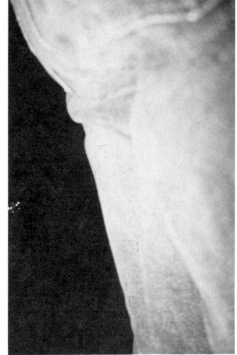

PHOTO: TOM DONGO

The Little UFO

PHOTO: VICTOR JOHNSON

This unknown flying object was photographed on four separate occasions. The authors feel that it is a craft of alien design and origin. We doubt that the U.S. government has this kind of technology.

The little UFO is about twelve inches wide and twelve inches tall and it is extremely powerful. Here is the reason why we say this:

In September 1994 Vic Johnson drove to an area a half mile south of the third portal area to do some nighttime videotaping, which was his practice at the time. He was in contact with Linda on his CB radio. At approximately 9 p.m. his pickup truck lost all power and would not start. Then the CB went dead.

Vic had little choice so he started walking out of the area in the dark. He was about halfway back and had the camcorder at the ready in case something happened. It did. He noticed a light a hundred yards away in the northern sky. The light was growing bigger because it was coming straight in his direction. Vic aimed the camcorder at the light and began filming. The camera's automatic focus locked onto the object as it drew closer. Vic got about six seconds of clear footage and then the camcorder went dead. The little craft has the power to shut down electronic devices and probably a lot more capabilities we aren't aware of. Vic walked back to Linda's location and as far as he can recollect he had no missing time.

PHOTO: TOM DONGO

PHOTO: TOM DONGO

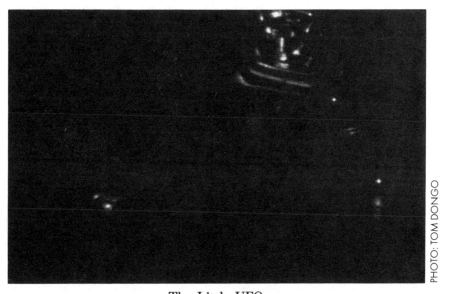

PHOTO: TOM DONGO

The Little UFO
— or something else —
very alien.

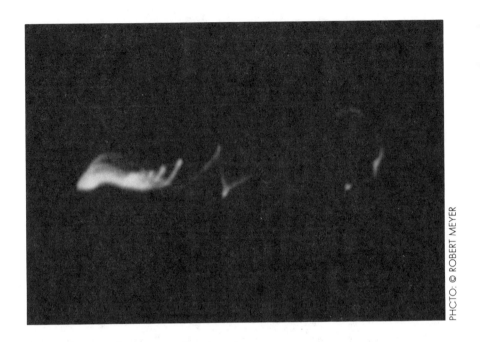

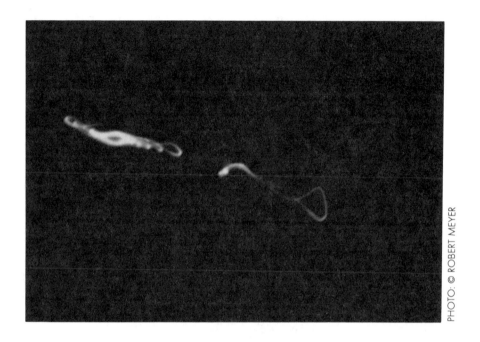

PHOTO: © ROBERT MEYER

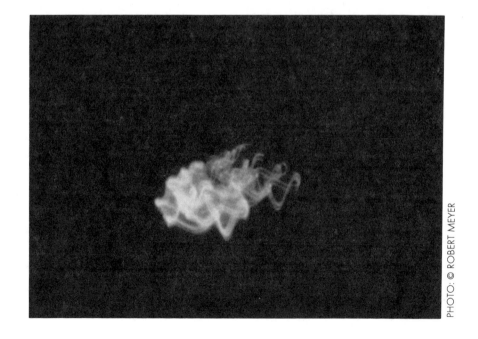

PHOTO: © ROBERT MEYER

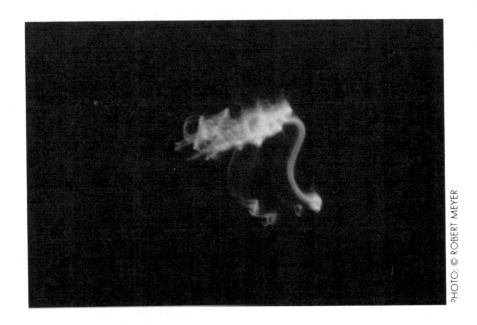

PHOTO: © ROBERT MEYER

The photographs on pages 186–188 are © Robert Meyer.

Robert Meyer's photographs are for sale.
For prices and catalogue, write to:

Celestial Light Creations
Robert Meyer
P.O. Box 10781
Sedona, AZ 86339-8781

PHOTO: TOM DONGO

This is a photo of two chrome/white UFOs that stopped in front of me after flying over Maroon Mountain in background.

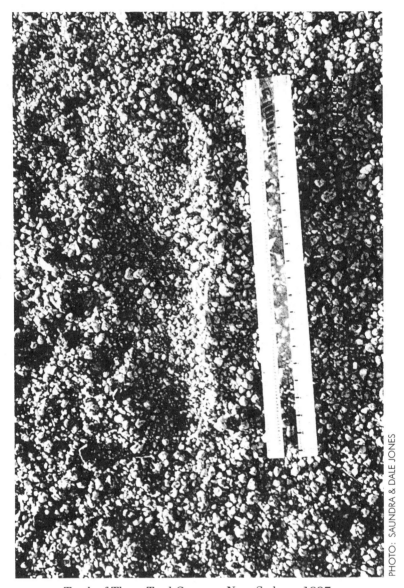

Track of Three-Toed Creature Near Sedona, 1997.

PHOTO: SAUNDRA & DALE JONES

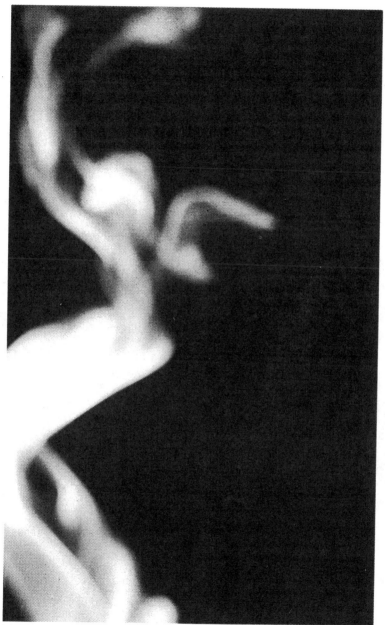

PHOTO: © BABETTE RENEÉ PROPPS, MAY 5, 2000, SEDONA, AZ, ALIGNMENT OF PLANETS NIGHT

This photo was hand delivered to a NASA laboratory in Houston, Texas. This photo is currently being taken seriously by several NASA scientists. Perhaps unofficially. The results may be quite interesting.

Photo taken near Sedona in 1998

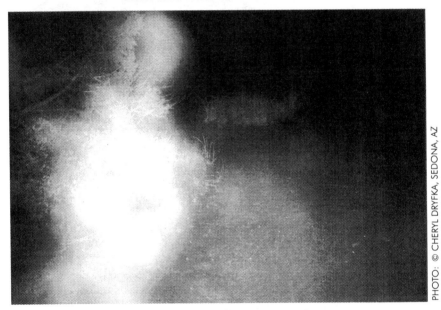

Photo taken near Sedona in 1998

Photo of Travis Walton at the 1995 International
UFO Congress.

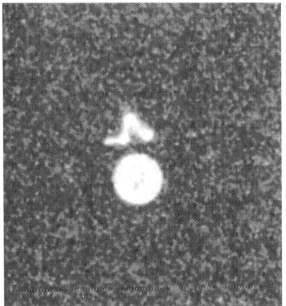

"Global Pulse
Probe."
Photo taken in
1998.

PHOTO: ANTHONY ALAGNA

California Halloween party 1996.

PHOTO: VICKIE McARTHUR

PHOTO: CHERYL DRYFKA

Photo taken near Sedona in 1998.

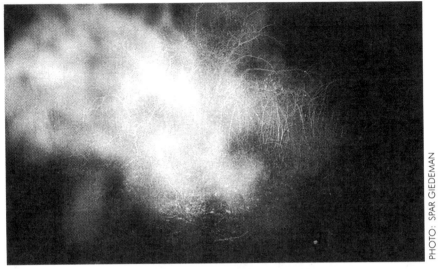

PHOTO: SPAR GIEDEMAN

Photo taken near Sedona in 1998.

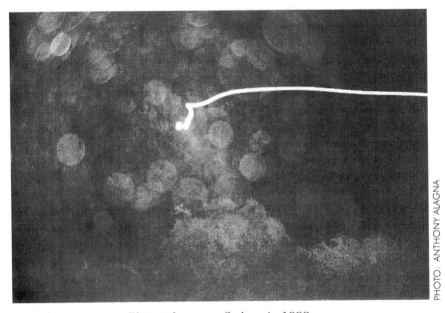

PHOTO: ANTHONY ALAGNA

Photo taken near Sedona in 1998.

Photo Section

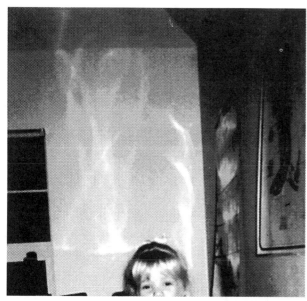

PHOTO: DIANE WARREN

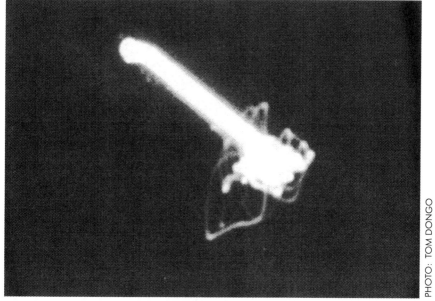

PHOTO: TOM DONGO

Photo taken near Sedona in 1996.

Merging Dimensions

PHOTO: GLORIA REISER

Photo taken in Boynton Canyon in 1990.

Photo Section

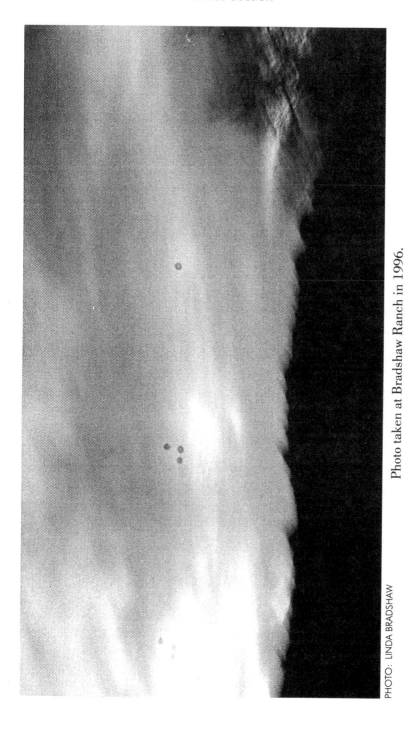

Photo taken at Bradshaw Ranch in 1996.

PHOTO: LINDA BRADSHAW

199

1995 UFO Congress, Mesquite, NV. Rubin Clinger and Tom Dongo.

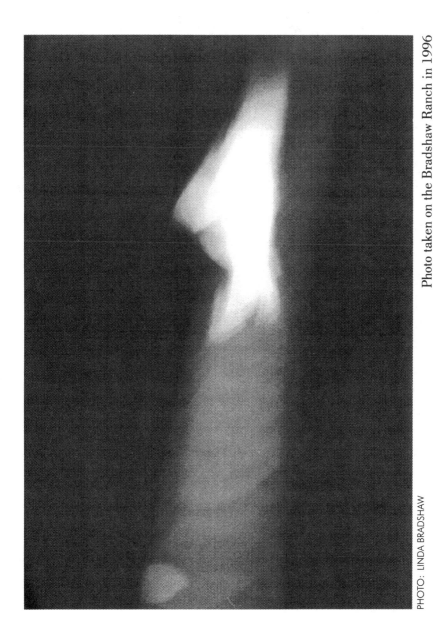

Photo taken on the Bradshaw Ranch in 1996

PHOTO: LINDA BRADSHAW

PHOTO: ANONYMOUS

Photo Section

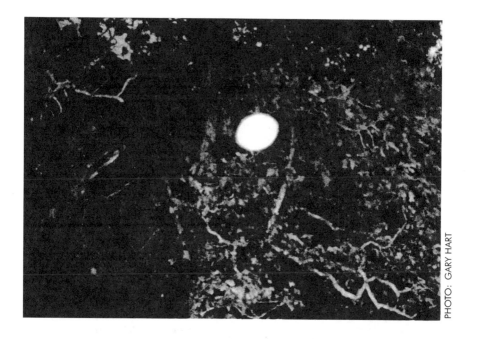

PHOTO: GARY HART

ORDERING BOOKS BY TOM DONGO
Autographed copies

__Everything You Wanted to Know
    About Sedona In a Nutshell. . . . . $4.95 $_____

__Merging Dimensions . . . . $14.95 $_____

MYSTERIES OF SEDONA SERIES:

__Book I — The Mysteries of Sedona . . . . $6.95 $_____

__Book II — The Alien Tide. . . . . $7.95 $_____

__Book III — The Quest. . . . . $9.95 $_____

__Book IV — Unseen Beings, Unseen Worlds . . $9.95 $_____

__Book V — Mysterious Sedona . . . . $9.95 $_____

Please include first class postage & handling as follows:
$3 for the first book, $1 each book thereafter. . . . . $_____

TOTAL ENCLOSED $_____

These rates apply to the U.S.A. Only. For orders outside the U.S., please write for rates.

Name _____

Address _____

City _____ State ____ Zip _____

Send your check or money order to:
Mysteries of Sedona, P.O. Box 2571, Sedona, AZ 86339

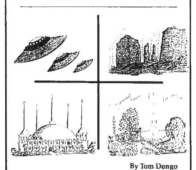

FROM TOM DONGO

MYSTERIOUS SEDONA

YEAR 2000 EDITION

TOM DONGO

ORDER TODAY

ORDER FORM IN THE BACK OF THIS BOOK

ALSO AVAILABLE

Mysterious Sedona

Contents

It is well-known among the curious that Sedona, Arizona, and its surrounding regions has seen some of the world's all-time most intense UFO, paranormal and spiritual activity.

The question is, why?

This book explores deeply into that enigmatic activity.

"Tom Dongo has captured the essence of the UFO experience in *Mysterious Sedona*. As I read the firsthand reports of his repeated meetings with this bizarre phenomenon, I could actually feel his astonishment, fear and wonderment. This marvelous book masterfully combines the themes of horror and science fiction and would make a great novel, except for one fact . . . it is all true."
— Peter A. Gersten, attorney and director of Citizens Against UFO Secrecy

"The book you are about to read is a collection of TRUE "high strangeness" experiences that have happened to people in or around Sedona, Arizona. It is a great read and a worthy addition to any library! Many of these stories are accounts that the author, Tom Dongo, has lived through. For events in which he was not a first-person participant, Tom has researched the facts and verified (where possible) each story from multiple sources. I also wish to tell you that I know the author, and I do assure you that Tom is an honest man who is only looking for truth. And, to the best of Tom's significant ability, you will find only truth within the pages of this book."
— Robert L. Dean, Founding Director, International UFO Congress

"Tom Dongo continues to amaze us with reports of strange airborne lights and vehicles, alien photos, mysterious men in underground tunnels, Bigfoot, and even a Sai Baba connection. I think Sedona has long been a place where odd souls are pushed, because there's a new paradigm is being born."
— Donald M. Ware, Bredveeder (and Colonel, U.S. Air Force, Retired)

"This is certainly an eye opening and comprehensive report on the Sedona mysteries for anyone interested in the high-strangeness phenomena going on there."

$9.95   ISBN 0-9622748-6-0

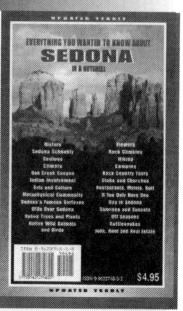